ADWYNNA MACKENZIE

Carefree, It Starts With Open

An Invitation to Come Out of Hiding and Embrace Your Super Natural Self

Copyright © 2019 by Adwynna MacKenzie

All rights reserved. No part of this publication may be reproduced, stored or transmitted in any form or by any means, electronic, mechanical, photocopying, recording, scanning, or otherwise without written permission from the publisher. It is illegal to copy this book, post it to a website, or distribute it by any other means without permission.

Adwynna MacKenzie asserts the moral right to be identified as the author of this work.

Adwynna MacKenzie has no responsibility for the persistence or accuracy of URLs for external or third-party Internet Websites referred to in this publication and does not guarantee that any content on such Websites is, or will remain, accurate or appropriate.

Designations used by companies to distinguish their products are often claimed as trademarks. All brand names and product names used in this book and on its cover are trade names, service marks, trademarks and registered trademarks of their respective owners. The publishers and the book are not associated with any product or vendor mentioned in this book. None of the companies referenced within the book have endorsed the book.

First edition

Cover art by Anne Mitchelson

This book was professionally typeset on Reedsy.
Find out more at reedsy.com

For Meaghan and Connor

Before you were born, someone asked me what I wanted for my children. I remember clearly my reply; "I want them to be healthy, happy, and allowed just to be."

I had no idea I had to be that first.

Thank you for being the motivation for me to become me. You are the lights that shine brightest in my world, and I am beyond grateful we chose each other to share this human experience.

Contents

Foreword — iii
Introduction — v
Prologue — xvi

I Being Carefree

Signs — 3
Flow — 7

II Before Carefree

Introducing: My Old Self — 13
The Lost Decade — 19
Digging In — 26

III Becoming Carefree

3D Creation – Climb Every Mountain — 35
Is That an Egg? - Wednesday, April 29th — 41
Observer - Thursday, April 30th — 46
Grace - Friday, May 1, 2015 — 55
Focus- Saturday, May 2, 2015 — 65
Miraculous - Sunday, May 3, 2015 — 70
Joyous Beyond Condition — 78
The Absence of Fear is Peace-Monday, May 4, 2015 — 88

IV   Beyond Carefree

What Are You Open To?	99
Dancing on Both Ends of the Stick	105
Rear-Ended Blessing	111
Parallel Lives	117
Alone on the Planet	122
What To Do When a Tiger Walks Into Your Meditation	128
The Song of your Soul	139
Truth Evolves	146
Who Am I Now?	153
Epilogue	162
Gifts & Gratitude	164
Notes	167
About the Author	170
Also by Adwynna MacKenzie	172

Foreword

This book, the one you have in your hands right now, is your invitation to come out of hiding and be who you've always wanted to be.

Maybe you're stuck. Or scared. Or worried about what others might think.

If you're like me, you've probably given up on yourself on numerous occasions. Taken detours. Made excuses to stop. But you keep coming back.

Because you know, deep in your heart, there is more to you than you've been allowing yourself to be.

I met Adwynna at a Dr. Joe Dispenza Advanced Workshop in Carefree, Arizona. It wasn't surprising we gravitated towards each other. We got to bond over our frustrations: businesses we hated, health issues that were "only going to get worse," and dreams so deeply buried we'd need to hire an archeologist to dig them up. We also discovered that we were curious, love Mexican food, and had a desire to have more of an impact in the world.

I was committed to writing every single day; something Adwynna found inspiring. I've turned that habit of writing into a new career with a best-seller called *Every Single Day,* and authored or co-authored eighteen books.

As she shares about in *Carefree, It Starts With Open*, Adwynna began having mystical experiences and profound insights. As the workshop progressed, I watched her become happier, lighter, more playful.

And then she took that home.

In her book, she says, *"I honestly, and somewhat naively, believed everyone would want what I had."* Some did, some didn't. I did.

Since those days in Carefree, we've become friends and co-creators. She's gained confidence her abilities. She sees what others can't easily see, guiding them to access who they are. She's a natural teacher, a compelling storyteller, and forever a student, too.

Navigating your new world takes courage and commitment. This book captures Adwynna's awakening, and also talks honestly about what it's like to live as her new self. How she found her footing on solid ground, while staying open to all that was unfolding.

It Starts With Open is only the beginning. It's the first book in the *Carefree* series and a first step towards the person you've been longing to become. Or maybe it's a baby step into the person you haven't dared to imagine yet.

If there's only one concept for you to take away from this book, it's this:

The end is no longer the goal.

The question is no longer, "What will I have achieved when I've completed this journey?" It's, "Where and when and how does my journey start?"

And because the universe arranged for me to meet Adwynna, I know the answers.

It starts with you.
  It starts right now.
  It starts with open.

Bradley Charbonneau, 2019, The Netherlands

Introduction

You have no idea how what you're doing today, by overcoming yourself and choosing a greater version of you, who you will help in some future time. Because you will be the truth, people need to see the living example of truth.
   Dr. Joe Dispenza

What do you think of when you read the word Carefree? Skipping lightly over the earth, picking a fluffy dandelion, and blowing the seeds into the wind? Maybe it's a state of mind you've never really had, or last recall when you were a child, open to exploring, just for the fun of it.

For me, Carefree is a place, a workshop, and the state of being I experienced as a result of attending said workshop in said place.

I literally walked in as one person and walked out as another.

What caused such a profound and permanent transformation? How did a stressed, depressed person who had given up on most of her dreams morph into someone who felt so free she was giddy with delight over simply being alive?

How did deep fears from childhood magically vanish, never to return? What doors flew open, plunging her into a vast universe filled with mystical encounters, resulting in superpowers beyond her wildest imaginings?

Apparently, it's called a spiritual awakening.

Why I Wrote This Book

It took a couple of years before I discovered there were names for what had happened to me. Learning there were labels for it was interesting because I honestly didn't give much thought to explanations when it happened, nor did I believe I was unique. Rather than researching the heck out of it, I leaned in further. I wasn't analyzing it; I was too busy living it.

While living it, I started to share my stories with people, which encouraged them to tell me theirs. I started gathering incredible tales of everyday courage and transformation, commingled with unrealized dreams, poor health, and a ton of pent up desire to be more and do more. We want our lives to have impact and meaning.

The most common request I get is, "tell me more about your mystical experiences." Why? Because people have had them too and don't know how to put them into words. They want to understand the meaning. They want more of them, yet they are also apprehensive. When we talk, they're relieved to discover they aren't crazy. They feel heard and understood, often for the first time in their lives. By the end of our conversation, they're excited to connect with their intuition so they can start trusting their guidance.

***

To make my story relevant for readers, I used the following questions as a guide for what made it out of my journals and into this book:

1. What would the Adwynna of four or five or even ten or twenty years ago want to know?
2. What would have helped me the most at various stages of my life?
3. What small thing, if I'd heard it and taken it in, could have saved me a few years, heck decades, of confusion, frustration, and misery?
4. How can the experiences I've had, the changes I've ingrained in my brain and body, the lifetime of learning and living that add up to the me of today, help the you of today?

Carefree, It Starts With Open packs in how I did what I did, what I've learned, and stories from the fabulous people I've met along the way. And it really is only the beginning! Stories are one of my favorite parts of being human, and collecting them to share with others is my life's purpose. It is my heartfelt desire that authentically told stories will inspire each of us to create healing, magic, joy, laughter, and fun in our daily lives.

How This Book Is Structured

My story begins in Part I, offering a glimpse of how it feels to live in alignment and flow. To answer the questions, "Does the magic continue once you leave the workshop?" "Are the changes permanent?"

Part II explains who I was going into Carefree. I'll tell how, despite many years of personal development training and inner work, I hadn't been able to overcome my deepest fears and traumas.

Part III explores the spiritual awakening itself. We watch as it unfolds, gaining insight into how it set itself in motion. As I discovered when writing this book, there were precise moments when I made choices that led to each breakthrough. Those moments, when carefully examined, teach us the value of making deliberate choices in our lives, while surrendering to the outcome.

In Part IV, I'll describe what it's like to leave the workshop and go into a world that feels very different then it used to. A lot like getting your land-legs after being on a ship for a week! I include some stories of other people who have undergone similar transformations so that you can start to see what is possible for you.

Each Chapter contains a story or experience, with excerpts from journals that capture the details and emotions as they occurred. All excerpts are unedited, dated, and offset in italics, so they are easily identified. Chapters end with a segment called, *Who Am I Now?* These segments offer insights into how I changed from each experience, with the intention of awakening the brilliant light within you.

* * *

A book, a journal entry, or a blog post captures a moment in time with the understanding one has gained at the time of writing. By the time you read this book, each *Who Am I Now?* segment has, in all probability, evolved and, in some cases, been replaced by more levels of Who I Am Now. In the Chapter called *Truth Evolves*, I dive further into the concept of how our perspectives will change if we remain curious and open to boundless possibilities.

> ***I ask that you accept my truth from my level of awareness at the time of my writing, allowing truth for both of us to evolve.***

Agreed? Whew, that was easy! Thrilled you're still here.

The Many Meanings of Carefree

The word carefree is defined as "being free from anxiety or worry," and conveys a sense of happiness, buoyancy, cheerfulness and other easy-going feelings.

The Dr. Joe Dispenza (Dr. Joe) community uses location names when we talk about workshops we've attended. In the spring of 2015, I went to my first Advanced Workshop in Carefree, Arizona.

This means I use the word carefree as a place-name and a workshop, often interchangeably. It also captures how I felt as a result of attending Carefree (see what I mean?) Carefree is also the perfect name for a book series!

The Carefree workshop theme was *Becoming Supernatural*[1], which became the title of Dr. Joe's 2017 best-selling book. I refer to that book, and the work of other authors, so you have access to scientific explanations of what happened to me. Those references and bonus content can be found in Notes and at resources.adwynna.com

Coming Out of Hiding

By the time I got to Carefree, I was ready for change. I was done with the whole "normal" charade. I can't say I knew who the new me was going to be, but I certainly didn't like the me who landed in Phoenix, Arizona on April 28, 2015.

> *I was ready for the unknown. I had no idea just how ready the unknown was for me.*

The week I spent in Carefree was an unexpected adventure into a whole new world. I'd written in my journal on the flight that I felt like I had a stone in my heart, yet I was all in from the minute I landed. It was as if

I could sense the changes that were coming. My future self was calling me, already confident in who she was, waiting for me to catch up and become who I'd always wanted to be.

I wrote prolifically in the months after Carefree, due to an unlimited supply of energy. Many nights I'd wake refreshed after a short time in deep slumber, climb out of bed to meditate, write or walk outside in nature. My children had landscaping jobs that summer and got used to finding me in the wee hours of the morning meditating or writing at the dining room table.

Home again after the workshop, I quickly learned that not everyone wants to jump up and down with joy simply because I was suddenly in a perpetual state of awe and bliss. I honestly, and somewhat naively, believed everyone would want what I had. I was driven to share how everyone could change their life, be healthy, free themselves, and feel really, really good. There were the occasional references made to an over-indulgence of Cactus Kool-Aid!

Eventually, those around me (and that includes me) began to trust the consistency of my results, my happiness levels, and the changes in me as they integrated. Once my friends and family saw I'd come down from the mountain and I was still happy, still meditating and having many, many cool things happen in my life, they relaxed and became more curious about how I'd done it.

＊＊

So many of us are stuck or hurting or wondering if our mundane life is all there is. That was me in early 2014. We've been conditioned to believe the fantasy we see all around us in commercials, social media, news, and movies. Tales are told to us from birth and presented as reality. We're encouraged to compete because there aren't enough resources. Our culture rewards the people who struggle the most and work the hardest. Science teaches us it's natural to decline as we age, that achy joints and mysterious pains are normal. We blame our genes, or our hormones, for poor health or inadequate sleep.

We end up believing that life is a lottery where some people get the good stuff, and others don't.

Something about that fantasy brought out my inner rebel. What made me question everything? What made me refuse to buy into the status quo? When it felt like life punched me in the gut and then kicked me when I was down, why was I still open to seeing things differently? I assure you; I don't look at all like a rebel. I'm slim, white, blonde, and the mother of a boy and a girl. I have a college degree, walk my dog, play tennis, and live in a house in suburbia. I've also questioned commonly accepted things since childhood and have always been very open to any, and all, answers.

You've found your way here, so I'm willing to bet you're a bit of a rebel too. How do you know you're in the right place?

1. You refer to yourself as weird, woo-woo, or crazy.
2. Maybe you've been hiding your true self – perhaps under a bushel, in a jar, or deep inside a bowl of popcorn while binging on Netflix?
3. You secretly believe you have superpowers and are still figuring out where to find them.
4. There is no magic in your life, and you're finally asking, "Is this all there is?"

My only goal in these pages is to share my personal experiences, allowing people to take away whatever helps them have what they most want in their life.

You will discover I have been to many, many mystical places while living a seemingly ordinary, and by some definitions, incredibly tragic life. I felt judged as different or unusual, so I'd hidden my mystical side from most people.

Hiding who we really are is the cause of so much heartache on this planet. We crave intimacy and connection, yet we often believe we are inherently unworthy and unlovable.

> ***Wouldn't it be a relief to know you have a safe place to land, where you are cherished for your uniqueness and loved because you are love itself?***

What I Mean by Mystical Experiences

I use the term mystical to describe things that happen outside of routine, predictable life. I could give you a list of possible mystical experiences, but I've found that when people are looking for something with a label, they miss what's right in front of them.

> ***Why won't I use commonly accepted labels or refer to metaphysical texts?***

Because it was my not knowing that allowed the mystical experiences to happen in the first place. It was my naivety, this childlike wonder with a sense of playfulness that kept opening me to more.

It's not that I don't love to learn. I'm a voracious reader and a sponge for knowledge. For over 20 years, I've studied the art and science of change. I hold certifications in a variety of healing modalities, work one-on-one in client sessions, write, speak, and teach workshops.

With all that knowledge, I remain curious about two things:

1. How do people change?

2. How does that change become permanent?

These questions motivate me to examine things from varying perspectives and reach new conclusions continually, yet this book won't give you:

- 8 Guaranteed Steps to Enlightenment
- 10 Rules for Unleashing Your Superpowers
- 15 Brand New Laws of the Universe from a Spirit Guide who only talks to me

There are no steps, and there are no rules. I am not a person who would label something a law of any kind, let alone presume to label one for the universe! Yes, there is a logical way of progressing from a state of close-minded fear to open-hearted joy. I have no idea of the number of steps it might take for anyone, but I do know one thing for certain. It all starts with open.

Being open is a choice. In truth, our life is an accumulation of the choices we make. It helps us be more comfortable about making those choices when we know someone else has gone there first.

* * *

There are a bunch of things I'd completely forgotten about until I started going through my journals, and I don't have space to include it all here. There were magical journeys to other dimensions and places on earth I'd never heard of, only to have my daughter search the internet and find they do exist. I delve into my struggles to live as a human being with all I am now seeing, experiencing, and knowing.

After my awakening, I opened to more and more guidance and changed my approach to helping others. I love the art of crafting great questions and ask a lot of them! When I meditate or write or go through my days, I receive answers. As I evolve, the work I do with people evolves, resulting in powerful shifts and rapid transformation. I strive to facilitate simple processes that allow people to access their power, accept responsibility for their choices, and create a compelling version of their future self.

Over time, I saw that being open to guidance without a lot of analysis brought me more and more mystical experiences. First in meditations and client sessions, then in daily life. I learned how to access more knowing, to let myself go deeper and deeper, often letting go of the very thing I had just learned to know more. It took time, but I finally got to the point where I trust my guidance, my gut, my SELF, who is so much more than me.

A Guidebook to An Expanded Life

The Carefree series are guidebooks to an expanded life. An enticement to explore those possibilities that exist just beyond the edges of your current reality. Like all good guidebooks, there are places you will read about that you will choose not to go, places you will visit and never want to return to again, and places you will go that you love so much you will want to bring everyone with you the next time.

When you've made a career out of hiding your true self, there is nothing like the process of writing a work of transformational non-fiction! The level of profound personal growth has been way more challenging than I imagined. Some of the mystical things I write about will stretch your beliefs. They certainly stretched mine. And yet, people want to know about the mystical stuff.

> *They want me to share because it gives them permission to share.*

When I started to be who I am openly, so many beautiful souls opened their hearts to me. The result is a variety of fun, creative, connected relationships with people from all over the world. I am grateful for their acceptance, encouragement, and love. There truly is safety in numbers, and it's my belief there are WAY more of us…open minded, longing for deeper connection, ready to create fuller lives…then we are led to believe.

It's time for more of us to come out of hiding, embrace the spotlight of truth, and allow our hearts to shine. It starts with me telling my authentic story so you can tell yours.

It starts with open…

Prologue

There is a place. I will call it a place, although some might describe it as a state of being. This is a place where all we know and all we are as a human ceases to exist. It is still, serene and calm. It would feel like nothing if nothing were a feeling one could adequately describe. It also feels like everything, if everything were a feeling one could adequately describe. You cannot describe it until it is over, and you have returned to the world of noise, sight, smell, and emotion.

For when you are in it, you do not know you are there because your world and everything associated with it has simply stopped. You have no knowing of yourself, nor do you have any knowledge that mere seconds before you were …well…a different version of you.

And when you return from this place, you are forever altered.

I call this StillSpace[2]. My first shared experience of StillSpace happened during an impromptu session while standing in my kitchen in Canada. The client was a long-time friend, and we were doing a quick piece of work before her flight back to the USA. Her beloved aunt had died, and she'd attended the funeral. She typically hides behind the camera, but her family insisted she jump into a few shots since she hadn't been home in a while. A couple of those photos had hit her like a Mack truck. "I didn't know how big I was," she told me with tears pouring down her face, "look at the size of my arms!"

I am certified in a variety of energy healing techniques and was helping her move through this emotional turmoil. Suddenly, she said, "What just happened? Did you feel that?"

Indeed I had.

We both had chills and goosebumps, and although neither of us could describe it, we knew we had gone into a void of stillness and that something very magical had happened.

Three days later, she called me and said: "whatever you did, you need to bottle it and sell it to addicts." She was in a state of bubbly excitement, saying, "Adwynna, my mind is quiet! My mind is quiet! There are no voices in my head telling me horrible things about myself!" She described making easy choices around food, how calm she was looking after her children, and how amazing it felt to not have the addict's voice yapping at her. A voice that had tormented her for most of her life.

She was free.

Two days after that session and before the phone call, I was working with another client. She was fed up with not showing up as her authentic self. Her intention for the session centered around her stepping into the powerful person she knew she was. She stated clearly and emphatically how she was ready to embrace herself as a dynamic and gifted teacher, and she was prepared to live authentically from that day forward. Months later, she shared with me that she had been at her lowest point, ready to give up her successful business and get a job.

Somewhere in the middle of our time together, StillSpace happened again. It was longer this time, and I became aware of it as it was happening and could hold us there longer. This client is very highly attuned, and she and I both knew at that moment, her life would never be the same.

She was free.

I drove home in a state of wonder and gratitude. I felt complete. I knew in my being that if those two sessions were the only two pieces of work I ever did on this planet, it would be enough.

It was as if I could sense the tremendous ripple effect of approximately 24 seconds in time.

None of us knew where those ripples would take us, or what waves we'd created.

I did have an inkling the waves were going to be huge...
...for all of us.

I

Being Carefree

I never end up writing what I think I'm going to write about.
Which means I end up writing what needs to be written.
Adwynna's Journal Entry May 13, 2015

1

Signs

"It's 7:15 AM on a Monday morning. I am dancing in the light of joy."

Have you ever wanted confirmation you're on the right path? Ever asked for a sign that says, "this is exactly what you're supposed to be doing now?" Do you pay attention to the answers showing up all around you?

Within minutes of finishing the Prologue, I was astounded to be a participant in a most unexpected and joyous encounter with nature.

Everything we do is co-created. We are also a co-creation, and not only because our parents had sex. I am, as so many other teachers have said before me, a physical extension of the oneness of the universe. Yes, I'm sitting here typing and doing so from my collection of journals and recordings and conversations and experiences. Yet to say I wrote this alone would be utterly laughable. As you will soon discover, I've had so much help from this world and beyond, I can barely capture it all!

During my week in Arizona, nature started calling me, and it's never stopped. What I'd always assumed was a gift of my daughter's, turned out to also be a gift of mine.

Of course, it had always been that way; I just hadn't been paying attention.

Nature is one of the ways I connect to source; the earth, the universe, God…source goes by many names. Yet when we connect to it, names no longer matter. Source is *felt* the same way by everyone. The challenge is describing it to another human! For me, seeing a deer, a hawk, or a hummingbird prods me to stop and notice my connection to source.

* * *

I receive much guidance during meditations, what I call my inner work. Often nature and animals show up there too, though nature's way may not be your way. Some people get their feedback from the universe when they notice numbers, like 11:11's or 4:44's on a clock. Others may be more attuned to astrology or get their messages from reading the Bible, drawing an inspirational card, hearing the perfect song, saying daily affirmations, or the many, many other choices available to us.

All of these methods are external validations of what is going on for us in our inner world. And they are *all* perfect for the person who chooses them.

Every day in Carefree was an endless parade of something new from nature's bounty; a coyote walked directly in front of our car, then stopped to stare at us before ambling off, birds would burst into song from the trees when I arrived somewhere. I'd watch in the early morning from our balcony as the desert came alive, seeing wrens perched on yellow flowers atop Saguaro's and jackrabbits coming out for breakfast.

I had a chat with a bright red male cardinal who was talking to me from a bush about three feet from my face. I can still see his orange beak opening and closing. As I was deep in conversation, I heard Bradley's voice calling out, "Adwynna, Adwynna, wait for me!" I still equate seeing a cardinal with Bradley, or I think of him, and cardinals appear.

During one walk from the workshop to the condo, we watched from a safe distance as a large family of javelinas crossed the road. We did a lot of all-out laughing and soggy crying that week, so it wasn't a surprise to find ourselves giggling on the roadside watching an older male who was a few minutes behind the main herd. This elderly pig was puffing a bit, somewhat out of breath, and seemed to be saying, "wait for me, you disrespectful whippersnappers!" as the youngest ones scampered across the road, way ahead of him.

Now I pay attention to magical moments and eagerly anticipate the messages offered in my daily walks and meditations. These encounters have given me so many learnings, timely feedback, and tons of joy.

Who Am I Now?

A person who is more aware of the moment to moment opportunities to adjust my thoughts, and someone who has practiced those skills so diligently it's become second nature.

> ***When I pay attention to what is happening in my life, I get more of it.***

By the time I left Carefree, my body knew the intense feelings of love, freedom, and joy. A sense of playfulness and lightness was birthed in me, and I will always choose to have more of that.

Yes, life still gets messy!

Because I want more of what feels good to me, I take the time to appreciate each encounter, each part from a book that answers a question, each conversation with someone that opens my thinking to more of what is possible.

__Appreciation for those small, seemingly inconsequential moments is the key to the future we want to create.__

And, as I discovered in Carefree, creating a new, you is a lot easier when you start with a curious mind and an open heart.

2

Flow

There came a time when I stopped seeing her and started being her.

Journal Entry, November 3, 2017

I finished the Prologue in the early evening and walked downstairs while writing a chapter in my head. These stranger-than-fiction books contain many interwoven stories, and those stories include so many beautiful souls who are such a massive part of my life. Some play significant roles; some minor and some are bit players who may not even know they had an impact.

Standing in my kitchen feeling love and gratitude for all of them, excited to be in the flow of writing, I looked out the window and saw a beautiful doe in the strip of grassy field behind our back yard. I see deer there often, and the previous weekend had a remarkable encounter with a fawn who came right up to me while I was meditating by a tree.

The perfect June day was fading as I walked onto the back deck to observe the doe. She sensed me there, lifted her head, watching me. She decided I wasn't a threat and resumed munching some green grass. Our deck is up high, and I was in that beautiful place of stillness, connecting with her and loving that feeling.

Suddenly I heard a buzzing noise.

I didn't move a muscle even though it could have been a hornet by my ear! Instead, the buzz became a hum as a ruby-throated hummingbird began flying in and out and around my head. A gorgeous male of iridescent greens and blues, he would stop in front of my face hovering in mid-air, looking right at me from 6"-8" away. He would flit over a bit and hang again, staring at me as I stayed very still. I could hear the steady hummmmmm of his wings, and he was so close I could see every detail of this beautiful, curious bird. I loved that he kept tilting his head like he was checking me out.

As if to emphasize this was not a random occurrence, or perhaps because I was emanating joy and it wanted more of that, this visit to me on my deck happened not once, not twice, but three times! The second time he flew off, he landed on the feeder (my first time seeing one there all summer) about four feet away, then flew off and quickly came right back. He popped to the feeder where a female hummingbird joined him, and they flew off together.

I thought the show was over and went back to admiring the doe. Then one female hummingbird appeared before me again right in front of my face and started talking to me. She'd flit, and chirp and flit and chirp and I was having an oh-my-God, is this really happening moment.

I was in complete awe and smiling with pure bliss yet calm and serene at the same time.

These birds represent joy and the sweetness of life. Their hovering ability is an evolutionary marvel of the impossible becoming possible. Sweet feedback, indeed!

Who Am I Now?

> *When we take the time to understand how we created our experience, we appreciate our own part in the creation. Manifesting becomes easier and more fun, so we do more of what led to it. We feel worthy of what comes to us and more empowered.*

A few weeks before the eye-level hummingbirds, I'd asked the universe to up my nature encounters. I'd been going through a funky period in my life and decided to put more emphasis on deliberately creating specific things and have higher levels of intention in my daily meditations. When I use the word *things*, I mean experiences, actual physical stuff, plus shifts in health and energy.

Of course, I had forgotten about those intentions when the hummingbirds showed up. If we begin to analyze an experience when we're in it, said experience typically stops.

It is excellent to analyze later, though, so we can consciously create more.

Reading this story now, I see what I'd been practicing in my daily life. I'd aligned with the feeling of being in flow with my writing and was appreciating that flow and the people in my life. I see a lot of deer, but I didn't take the doe's visit for granted. I took the time to go outside and connect with her and enjoy her presence in the field. In that moment, I was fully present and content.

When you least expect it, the universe will surprise you with more than you've been asking for. Things will slip in through the crack of least resistance. How and when things show up *is* the surprise, and if you are wide open like I was on that summer evening, the surprise arrives as a cool, fun, and joyous hummingbird chatting in your ear from less than a foot away!

When I thought about it later, I'd been wondering where the

hummingbirds were. My husband had remarked on their absence the day before and commented that I might be disappointed they weren't at the feeder. I had replied, "Maybe they are feeding, and I'm just not there to see them when they do." Which means, I wasn't feeling disappointed. I knew they (what I wanted) were out there, and I had yet to allow them into my experience.

The more I play with all of this, the more the universe surprises me. And play is the right word here, although it took a significant breakthrough for me to understand that!

II

Before Carefree

"The quest for truth has many layers."

3

Introducing: My Old Self

We have to own our story before we can release it.
Journal Entry May 12, 2015

When we moved north of Atlanta, Georgia, from Toronto in late 1998, I was ready to change the world. In September of that year, I had my first experience of merging into Oneness. A friend had been using a "Light Machine" to induce trance as a way to help her write a book and encouraged me to try it. I remember going into the void of colored lights, emerging with a deep personal knowing we are all One.

From 1996-1998 I'd had some mystical experiences that began with a decision to leave corporate life. At the time, I was struggling with all aspects of my life. I had two very young children, a nanny, and a high paying job with many demands.

Plus, I was drowning in grief.

When my son Connor was ten months old, my younger sister and her unborn child were in a car accident. Dr. Tracey MacKenzie was rushing to get to a woman in labor, went off the pavement onto the gravel at the side of the road, over-corrected, went over two lanes, and sideswiped the median that divides the highway. She swerved to the side, only to have the complete misfortune of leaving the road at a large culvert, flipping her car upside down and landing in a boggy ditch. Although the doctors performed an emergency caesarian section, Tracey and her much loved and anticipated daughter both died.

The agony of losing them both was multiplied by the feeling of being singled out for a life of unjust pain. My older sister had died of complications from asthma about ten years earlier in my final year of university.

On a gorgeous, sunny day in June 1994, I went from being a middle child to an only child.

During all the trauma, I discovered I was pregnant with our second child. It felt like a miracle, and it also felt like way too much to handle. I knew instantly it would be a girl. My daughter, Meaghan, arrived in a spring snowstorm in April 1995 and is strong, beautiful, powerful, gifted, and brilliant.

* * *

By the spring of 1996, Meaghan was almost a year old, and I was living a gray-scale life. I had left the corporate world, lured by the promise of becoming a trainer who would inspire others. My new boss told me everyone who worked with them had to have something called a New Decision Therapy™ (NDT) session. So off I went.

NDT is a forgiveness technique developed by Dr. Kandis Blakely in the 1980s and was built on the work of Dr. John Diamond, M.D[3]., a pioneer of holistic healing. Using a step-by-step formula to pinpoint past traumas, NDT releases stuck emotions, freeing people from the chains of the past.

I wrote in June 1996 what I will say even now; in less than 15 minutes, I forgave my younger sister for dying and released the anger I had over her leaving us behind. When I woke up the next morning, my world was suddenly in technicolor. I could hear birds, I felt the joy of sunshine, and I knew I had to find out what had happened to me.

That started what I called "The Year of the WOW!" I threw myself into learning NDT, traveled to California to become a certified practitioner, and offered to organize events and certification workshops for Kandis.

I devoured even more books, took classes, started meditating, and my journals are chock full of AHA moments. I did bring NDT to Canada, filling workshops for Kandis, writing her manuals, and organizing speaking engagements and book signings. I became an Instructor and started seeing a full roster of clients, speaking at events, and teaching workshops.

Eventually, Kandis, who was now my close friend and mentor, became my business partner, and we formed NDT International. We wanted to expand the work, take it to more countries, and help more people. I saw my future as a teacher and a healer.

During my mystical Light Machine trip into oneness, I felt love I didn't know existed. I'd been delighted to discover something contrary to my mentor's teaching; there is no hierarchy. No soul is more advanced than another.

This was a massive revelation. My *not- good-enoughness* vanished. I knew in my core that no one would walk around in human form, proclaiming themselves to be an old soul or enlightened master. To do so would imply they are more evolved, and therefore better than someone else.

A true master believes we are all masters.

I was so excited to share my new insights with Kandis! She arrived in Toronto a few weeks later to teach workshops I'd put together for her. I was high, vibrating at a new frequency, and I wanted everyone to know they are all equally powerful.

After all, if we are each a unique expression of the oneness, how could any one of us be more or less powerful than the other?

When we change, the people around us poke us to see if we're real. And I got poked big time! The student was proclaiming herself equal to the teacher, and the teacher was not happy. Our visit was strained, and our practitioner community was confused and dismayed to see Kandis publicly demeaning me.

* * *

Moves are all-consuming and even more so to another country. In Atlanta, we bought an enormous new home in a friendly neighborhood of equally large homes. We were welcomed immediately and began a life full of parties, tennis, and kid's activities. I used those first months to do Mom things and figure out what to do next.

Within six months of moving, my friendship and business partnership with Kandis was over. The vision I had for my life was ripped apart in a garbled phone message from her that was filled with anger over money.

A few days later, I opened my mailbox to a greeting card written before the phone message. In it, Kandis sweetly proclaimed her love for me and explained she needed to run things her way. I plunged further into despair. With one paragraph, she dissolved the bonds of friendship and a business I'd envisioned growing into an organization of practitioners healing people all over the world.

We never communicated again.[4]

Who Am I Now?

It took me a very long time to heal from my relationship with Kandis. We'd been so close, our business and personal lives intricately entwined. One of my startling discoveries was the discovery that my self-esteem was so low when we'd first met that I'd swallowed her whole.

I hadn't wanted to be like _her, I had wanted to_ be _her._

Even though I grew during our time together as mentor and mentee, my belief in my own power, my ability to bring in divine work, and take it into the world was latent, hidden beneath a lifetime of faking self-confidence.

I later came to understand that I deferred to her because she claimed to hold a higher vibration than the rest of us. I viewed her as unique, a chosen one, someone who could receive direct information from the higher realms. She was the guru, and I felt connected to it all because she was my friend. When she pulled the plug, I became even more lost than the first day I'd sat in her class. Plus, now I had betrayal, resentment, and mistrust to add to my daily dose of not feeling good enough.

For a few years after our breakup, it seemed the deeper I dove into the spiritual world, the more disappointed I became with the teachers. One day, while standing in a bookstore wondering whether to purchase the book in my hand, I shared that disappointment with the store owner. He gently advised me to learn from the message and be forgiving of the messenger.

This timely advice allowed me to find compassion for another person's journey and accept their growing pains along the way. Advice

I still apply to myself. It also allowed me to continue filling myself with information. I devoured books, and then the internet started to kick in with videos. For the next decade or more, I poured knowledge into my mind. I prided myself on my mental acuity and loved all the information I was accumulating.

I was looking outside of myself for everything, including my self.

4

The Lost Decade

"Do not discount your suffering; it's as much a part of your journey as the joy."
Meaghan Horsley

When we returned to the Toronto area in 2004, I didn't seek out my previous healing community. Instead, I embarked on what I jokingly refer to as the lost decade.

It's so lost let's smush it all into one paragraph. Here are as many excuses for me not being me as I can possibly muster:

> The kids were young, the move was sudden and stressful. We had plucked them from their happy life and moved where they knew no one. We had a new house to finish and new schools, activities, and things to organize. The kids were in high-level sports, and I needed the flexibility to get them to games and practices. My husband was uncertain about what he wanted to do and went through a

bunch of jobs. He tried to transfer some of the pressure he felt to me. Which meant he wanted me to go back to work and make money. I'd been out of the regular workforce for years. I didn't want to restart my healing practice because how I'd been trained no longer felt authentic. I convinced myself I wasn't qualified to do much anymore. I knew I could always do sales or admin work so I'd get a contract or a job, give it my all and then feel overqualified, unappreciated and resentful. My husband and I had an unspoken agreement that only one of us could do what they really wanted at a time because the core belief was you couldn't make money and be happy doing it. I tried to make him happy, yet I wanted freedom. I felt like we had more than enough already and could get by with less, if we just chose happiness over money. He resented me. I resented him. He became depressed. I became depressed. He hid it. I hid it. Stress mounted. I knew stress depletes your energy and leads to disease, yet I couldn't stop the spiral.

To the outside, though, we looked like the perfect family.

In the beginning, like everyone else who is fed up and ready for change, I wanted the pain to stop. Whether our suffering is from conflict, disease, stress, or misery, most of the time, we want to change because we are uncomfortable.

* * *

There are way too many people telling us we have to live with IT (whatever IT is). You will have IT for the rest of your life, IT is a sign of your age, IT is because of your genetics, and my personal favorite; IT is because of your mother!

My pain wasn't evident to most people, yet the mental torment I went through was all-consuming at times. There were days I wanted to get in the car, point it in any direction, and just drive until I ran out of road. My love for my children held me together, along with this reassuring voice that kept telling me, "all things are possible."

* * *

Results from a saliva stress test in early 2014 confirmed my overwhelm, poor sleep, digestive issues, and general weariness. People sometimes call this adrenal burnout, as the adrenal glands are responsible for our responses to stress.

> *Levels of the main adrenal hormone, cortisol, rise, and fall in a daily pattern that underlies the more erratic fluctuations caused by the stress response. Cortisol output by your adrenal glands is one of the most reliable indicators of your adrenal function and how well your body is dealing with stress. The Cortisol/DHEAS Saliva Test measures the levels of the stress hormones DHEAS and cortisol in your saliva and provides an evaluation of how cortisol levels differ throughout the day.*[5]

My cortisol readings were so erratic and low by mid-afternoon that the doctor presenting my results actually asked me how I managed to get through my days without collapsing in exhaustion by 3 o'clock! I agreed to a supplement and diet protocol that started when I woke up and ended with taking something before bedtime. Not only was it costly, but it was also time-consuming, and there was no real end in sight.

After a few months of constantly being beeped by my cell phone to pop something, I was fed up. I felt better, but not vibrantly healthy. Plus, I knew there was a better way. I knew our bodies have the innate ability to heal, and I was frustrated.

How could I tap into that ability?

* * *

In mid-July, I picked up a magazine at my parent's house that had Dr. Joe on the cover. I read the article, immediately ordered his book, *You Are the Placebo*[6], and devoured it like a summer novel. I recall my family asking me what I was reading as I shooed them away to make their own dinner. Already plotting out how I could get to a Progressive Workshop.

Even though that article arrived months after I'd put my frustrated question out there, I see how I was open to receiving a way to heal that did *not* include a lifetime of supplements and dietary restrictions.

I certainly hadn't asked for the solution to be meditation, nor had I heard of Dr. Joe, even though he hangs out with scientists and authors I've followed for years.

When you're open, the universe delivers more than you expect.

* * *

I'd been so enthusiastic about a Progressive Workshop, but I did my very best to sabotage getting to one. My friend, Jeannie, booked it and I didn't, but I had the hotel room. The workshop sold-out while I procrastinated, so I had to beg the staff to let me in. It's actually funny to look back on now. I drove for eight hours in snow, rain, and sleet to get there along with many loud, obnoxious voices in my head. My Monkey Mind was a relentless barrage of :

- *You've done this before.*
- *This won't work.*
- *How long will this last even if it does work?*

I did warn the voices; this might be their last chance to drive me nuts, so they really made the most of it.

Three days later, I drove home in the joy of a bright sunny day, and immediately signed up to go to Carefree.

> *November 2014 Post Progressive Workshop-Journal Entries*
>
> *I have been shocked by the VAST amounts of rage, anger, and resentment in my body. Stuck in my throat as unspoken wrath. Really vicious and awful. During the workshop, when I did The Breath, stuff would leave my body along with swear words - really, bad ones - words I didn't think I even knew!*

* * *

> *I woke up in the night with an old shoulder/rib injury flaring up and then an hour later had a horrible sore throat. The throat felt like the time I had an abscess on my tonsil. Both were gone by morning. I guess crap leaves in odd ways.*

* * *

The Progressive was the first time I'd ever done anything like the breathing technique Dr. Joe describes in Chapter 5 of *Becoming Supernatural*. As *The Breath* moved up my body and into my head, all these nasty words would be blasting away in my brain. Often, the energy making its way up would get stuck in my throat from a lifetime of stifled words and unexpressed emotions.

Old emotions and buried traumas were starting to leave my body. It wasn't pretty, but the relief of release brought me a new sense of well-being and, most of all...hope.

No one's journey to wholeness is a straight line.

Who Am I Now?

Hindsight truly is a beautiful thing. In the middle of the lost decade, I most definitely did *not* see my presence in any organization I was working for as being particularly beneficial. I was typically brought in to fix something because I have a diverse skill set, an ability to learn just about anything, and a strong need to be needed.

By the way, the latter will make you say yes when you need to be answering no.

Despite my many diversions, I don't believe any of those choices was a mistake. As things have played out over time, I've discovered that the people I worked with ended up with stronger visions for their lives and their organizations. As did I.

* * *

In late 2014 I made a list of the things I was grateful for since the Progressive Workshop. The ones here would have been more than enough to receive from an investment of time and money from a weekend. Plus, the gifts that began then, just keep on giving.

- *I can now bend, look up and down without feeling headachy or nauseous. This means I can garden, clean, organize, and decorate my Christmas tree without puking!!*
- *I have energy, focus, and can get through my days without feeling exhausted.*
- *I have actually stopped obsessing over (insert name(s) here) who used to drive me bonkers!*
- *I also experience bizarre episodes of quiet and look around, wondering where all the noise has gone. It's not no noise in my house, it's no noise in my head!*
- *My continual, endless, ridiculous, agonizing chatter is often gone. Like weird empty space - waiting for inspiration.*

* * *

My husband once asked me, "What do you get from all this meditating and Dr. Joe stuff?" I took a deep, calm breath and let the answer fall out of my mouth...

"A quiet mind."

5

Digging In

It's a short journey back to how things were. Unless I choose otherwise. I choose otherwise.
   Journal Entry June 5, 2015

2015 was the longest, coldest winter we'd endured in a long time with massive snowbanks and sub-zero temperatures. Our welcome break was a vacation to Aruba, with four other couples and a big house for ten days of sunsets, warmth, parties, beaches, laughter, games, and way too much alcohol. Aruba is a tiny island with very little to explore. It's ridiculously windy all the time, so golf and tennis were out of the question unless your idea of a great golf outing is $250 per round, while watching your ball head in the direction of Venezuela.

* * *

I was reading Dr. Joe's *Breaking the Habit of Being Yourself*[7] and had committed to doing the exercises in the book for once. I'm a prolific reader, just wasn't a prolific doer of the exercises included in many personal development books.

Chapter 7 in *Breaking the Habit* altered the course of my life. It's called *The Gap*, and I can quote the opening paragraph from memory, "I was sitting on my couch one day, thinking about what it means to be happy. As I contemplated my utter lack of joy, I thought about how most people who were important to me would have given me a pep talk right on the spot." wrote Dr. Joe, "…to me something wasn't right."

Maybe it was the timing, who knows? The week before, I'd had a freakily similar conversation with a friend using many of those same words. That friend had given me said pep talk, and yet I also knew "something wasn't right."

This was a man who was on top of the world by exterior measures. He was becoming more and more sought after to speak to audiences after a movie called *What the BLEEP do we Know*? He had a loving family, a beautiful home, he helped people heal in his clinic and had enough wealth to live a comfortable life. He was also acutely aware that the only time he felt truly alive and happy was when he was on stage. Offstage he wasn't that person. That was his *Gap*.

While I wasn't well known, I was a writer, I'd once been a teacher and a speaker, I was helping people in profound ways. Yet I wasn't openly sharing or pursuing what I'd wanted to do since I was five years old.

Then I read how Dr. Joe retreated from his life for six months. He stopped lecturing, which many people thought was nuts. He wrote, "I didn't want to lecture again until I was the living example of everything I was talking about."

At that moment, I knew I'd finally found a teacher I could trust.

It took Dr. Joe six months to close his gap, and he shared in *Breaking The Habit* how he did it and how I could do it too. Turns out, he was considering leaving public life during that time.

The combination of the committed and passionate man I'd seen at the Progressive Workshop and the man who was willing to walk away from a seemingly perfect life spoke directly to my broken heart. Was this a teacher who had lived through the same things his audience was living through? Was this man, who stood at the front of the room and talked about his struggles, his daily habit of overcoming himself, his desire to understand what he may not be seeing, what he might be missing, finally be the real deal?

* * *

I have always disliked the "teach what we most need to learn" mantra delivered to people who want to teach, speak, and inspire others. While I understand we are always learning and growing, I want to know you've made it through the fire and emerged stronger before you tell me to trust you and walk into the flames! As much as I loved Dr. Joe's science, what I really wanted was an authentic teacher, someone who was committed to me becoming...well...me.

You see, years ago, I'd vowed never to teach someone else what I didn't know for sure. And certainty comes from personal experience. Reading *The Gap* made me realize I had to become the person who had walked through the fire and could stand with confidence in my own light...or I would never set foot on a stage.

To realize my deepest dreams meant I needed to take a good, honest look at who I was being.

This translated into doing the exercises in the book, starting to meditate regularly again and making some decisions around dismantling my old identity to allow the new me, the truth of me, to emerge.

* * *

These are excerpts from my exercises from the chapter in *Breaking the Habit* called *Prune Away the Habit of Being the Old Self*.

Dr. Joe asks questions for us to contemplate: What kind of person have I been? What type of person do I present in the world? What part of my personality do I need to work on improving? We have a choice to unmemorize an emotion that conditions us and really dig into how that is showing up for us.

So I dug in…

02/18/2015 Journal Entry Aruba

> *I have been brave in thought, but not always in action. I present a confident, competent, and organized face, yet feel overwhelmed, out of control and disorganized on the inside. I know the need to have a vision, goals, and a plan but cannot make myself write down something as small as a daily to-do list.*
>
> *I am an exceptional, intuitive, calm, and accepting healer, but do not extend that graciousness to myself. I am a hard and unrelenting critic of my own life and behaviors.*
>
> *I way too often modify or diminish myself to make others feel better. I am constantly on guard for any discord.*
>
> *I have very high expectations for myself and berate myself when I fail for not knowing more, better, or sooner.*

I wanted to learn to let go and create my own flow. And then I found it, the emotion underneath it all.

Resentment.

Resentment was ugly to me. After all, how could I resent when I had so much in my life? Yet there it was staring back at me from the page. All the time's other people got love, invitations, promotions, or attention.

It didn't matter how good I was, how hard I worked. What I did and who I was just wasn't enough.

> *Resentment feels like a hand squeezing my heart, short of breath, tight in chest, coiled up guts. Ugh!*
>
> *My state of mind is competitive, blaming, overwhelmed, self-pitying, desperate, overly intellectual, lazy, deceptive, sensitive and insensitive, judging, self-important, short-tempered, and self-righteous.*

Resentment was blocking my ability to fully receive and truly feel all the love and great things I had in my life. Hiding it was exhausting, and so was continually trying to be what I thought others wanted me to be.

My early childhood had conditioned me into a perpetual state of stress from constantly monitoring the environment around me for danger. As I discovered in Carefree, this is a condition called Hypervigilance, which is a state of increased alertness often associated with Post-Traumatic Stress Disorder (PTSD).

Who Am I Now?

During my voyage of discovery from the exercises in *Breaking the Habit of Being Yourself*, I learned the next step was to begin to let go of my resentful old self and start to embrace a new me. And the new me needed to be created with as much energy as I had put into the old me. I had to want to become a greater version of myself more than I wanted to stay stuck in resentment.

That sounds so easy when I write it like that in one sentence.

Was it easy? Sometimes. Sometimes it was painful and hard and required me to look at parts of myself that I judged as being not all that pretty. Was it worth it? Absolutely. I wrote in February 2015 that I wanted *love, compassion, understanding, hope, admiration, patience, and happiness.*

Was it because I'd asked for states of being instead of specifics, like cars, money, or relationships, that I got so much more than I asked for? I'll never know for sure, but I suspect so.

III

Becoming Carefree

*Now, as I enter the Dr. Joe workshop,
I enter with a stone of cold-hearted terror embedded in my chest.
I know it is irrational and so not me.
But it is me.
That small person who believes she is unlovable.
So closely guarded, so buried, so very, very, very hidden.
Can I become compassion?
Can I discover and maintain calm-passion?
What I want ...*
Intention
Clarity
Mission
Focus
Power

Journal Entry on the plane to Phoenix, AZ April 29, 2015

6

3D Creation – Climb Every Mountain

April 29, 2015-Journal Entry

We just hiked Black Mountain. Jeannie, one of our new roomies and myself. Our roommate is gorgeous, young, fit, and she pretty much ran to what I thought at the time was the top of the mountain. **I'd only observed her journey from my own perspective.**

I didn't know she'd given up short of the top, or maybe just decided it wasn't worth it.

Jeannie's foot was hurting, and it was her first day ever in Arizona. She had her phone and was taking photos of everything along the way. Me - I'm striving for the top. Thinking about "sitting around" for the next 4-5 days, wanting to get some exercise.

I'm not totally unconscious- good God I'd never have made it through the event if I had arrived as my prior highly competitive type A high driver personality. Much of that had softened over the years of work I'd done.

I definitely wanted to get to the top but knew to pace myself-kind of slow and steady, taking time to stop and admire the view along the way. It was hot- there are these little flies- they don't seem to bite.

The view is spectacular, but I am connected to my inner voices and must make a conscious choice to breathe, admire, and notice my surroundings. It isn't natural... I didn't even know that was possible then.

My legs are like rubber, and the top keeps changing its location. It seems like it's right up there, and when I get there, there's more to go.

I find inner resolve and push myself past where my body wants to go.

I realize now this is a strength I needed later in the event. That push, that drive, that desire to push through to get to my perceived goal.

The funny thing is I hadn't really thought about what might be at the top. I just wanted to get there.

Especially when I passed my new roomie on her way back down, and she said she hadn't bothered to go all the way.

Extra incentive.

Push, breathe, strain.

There it is.

I ascend.

It sucks up there!

The breeze is gone, the air is hot.

The flies are so thick they are in my eyes and ears and mouth, covering my body as I flail at them.

There's no stop to admire the view. Two lovely Japanese girls take my photo and I take one of them too, so we can all say we made it.

Made it to what?

We couldn't scramble off that "peak" fast enough.

Beware of ill-conceived goals.

I met Jeannie on the way down. She is happy, she has beautiful photos, and has chatted up some nice people. She's in her element.

I'm laughing at myself for missing the journey-again!

It is the beginning of my journey in Carefree. It is another reminder of why I dislike traditional goal setting.

Too much emphasis on competition, push, strive, reach, grasp. Missing it all to get there fast...

* * *

Carefree introduced me to Fifth Dimensional (5D) creation, and I will admit it took me a long time to understand this intellectually. If you want to know more, read *Space-Time and Time-Space,* which is Chapter 11 in *Becoming Supernatural.* I certainly got Third Dimensional (3D) creation, or what Dr. Joe calls "changing matter to matter." 3D creation works; it just takes time, requires considerable effort, and doesn't allow for many fun surprises along the way.

It's also why so many of us feel flat once we reach our 3D goal.

Sort of like me on the top of Black Mountain. By the time I got there, I'd forgotten why it was so vital for me to reach the top. Did I even consider whether it would be pleasant up there on the pinnacle?

Nope.

I'd barely stopped to admire the view along the way, and I'd left my friend Jeannie behind. I sacrificed my health for a chance to stand alone in my victory, and my legs hurt so much, I could barely move for the entire workshop. To top it off, I'd also lost money, having tucked a $20 bill in my sock that was now floating somewhere in space.

Running downhill from the heat and the flies to a place where the breeze was fresh, I quickly realized the metaphors for my life and saw my deeply ingrained programming.

Great start to the workshop, and we'd not gone into the classroom yet!

* * *

I'd started working in high-tech corporate sales right out of college, was promoted into management, and then transitioned into the world of holistic health. Over the years, I've had tons of leadership training, and have many tools in my kit-bag. I'm proficient in muscle testing, which is a catch-all term for a technique with decades of clinical and practical usage. In a nutshell, muscle testing allows me to determine whether a statement is true or false. I use this technique to guide client sessions and assist in my own decision making.

To understand the history and many applications of muscle testing, I'd suggest reading the updated version of *Power vs. Force, The Hidden Determinants of Human Behavior by* David R. Hawkins.[8]

I've been helping people set S.M.A.R.T. goals[9] for years, and the process did not seem to result in happy, fulfilled lives. Sure, some people achieved their goal of standing on the top of the mountain along the way, yet many reported feeling emotionally flat instead of invigorated. Most often, though, I've found people lose the belief that their goals will be achieved and stop dreaming entirely.

That was me by 2014. I no longer trusted myself to make a goal that wouldn't result in me standing alone on a mountain top, hot, tired, barely able to breathe, swatting away annoying flies.

I knew in my being there was a more natural way, but I hadn't heard of 5D creation.

Who Am I Now?

I know everything matters. Every encounter. Every serendipity. No matter how small, each is moving us where our Higher Self knows we want to go. When people say "there are no coincidences," they really mean there are NO coincidences.

> *May 24, 2015-Journal Entry*
>
> *Outside planting flowers for my boxes and a spider climbed up the front of my shirt, over my chest, and hopped onto my arm. Made sure I saw him. No fear, just observation. I allow myself to be guided now. I stop what I am doing and go where I am guided. I use Muscle Testing (MT) all the time. Gives me massively more time in my day.*
>
> *When things come up for me, I clear them. This is the joy of having tools. I am "off" (meaning I have muscle tested, and the following statement was not true for me) for "I am at peace with myself whether anyone accepts me or not." This has to do with the final stages of me needing to be noticed, needing to be special. Needing outside love and approval.*
>
> *I had a belief that enlightenment or higher vibration means you will never fail again. That people will only love you in perfection, but not in failure.*
>
> *This belief does not give me permission to fail, and we will all fall from grace occasionally. It's recognizing, correcting, and apologizing that makes the difference.*
>
> *(I retest the statement and am now "on," meaning my truth is now, "I am at peace with myself whether anyone accepts me or not.")*
>
> *Spider is about Creativity & Weaving of Fate. The spiral of the web, converging at the center. Teacher of language, the magic of*

writing.

I weave a web of magic with the written word.

My integration from Carefree took many months, and I was so willing to look in every dark corner, face every part of me that stood in the way of me having the future I had created there. I'm grateful I had the tools to clear out negativity, and meditation to fill and empower me.

The way I did was very efficient. The tools I used then are openly available and easy to learn. [10] I still use many of the same tools, but my perspective is different now.

> *I used to look for an opening to remove negativity from the past. Now I look for openings into the life we want to create and align the energy to match that creation. It's a subtle shift in perspective that creates significant shifts for myself and my clients.*

7

Is That an Egg? - Wednesday, April 29th

An ethereal rainbow colored egg that glowed with an inner light.

The Carefree Advanced Workshop started on a Wednesday evening with Dr. Joe taking us through the next four days. I distinctly recall him explaining how we would be "creating something from nothing" or what he calls "dimensionalizing" an object, a new concept for me. We'd be learning how to bring something from 5D into our 3D reality. He was only setting up the exercise, yet my mind's eye kicked in right away. When he said to pick an object to dimensionalize, I immediately saw a gorgeous iridescent blue dragon egg. It was lit from within, and I was in love with it. Then he said to pick something ordinary, but not so common that it's everywhere.

I was a tad disappointed to admit that a dragon's egg might not be in the ordinary category, so I let that go, and then another egg popped into my mind. One plain brown egg. From a chicken!

All Advanced participants are asked to bring a completed Mind Movie[11] to workshops. A Mind Movie is what it sounds like. You make your own movie with photos, videos, music, and affirmations of the life you want to be living. AKA your *future self*, another term I would hear over and over in the Dr. Joe community. To keep the explanation simple, we would watch our movies during sections of the workshop to "install" what we wanted to create into our unconscious mind.

The cool part is discovering how our movies literally start coming to life.

I get such a kick out of the objects people choose to dimensionalize and how they finally appear. Sometimes it takes time, and sometimes it happens during the workshop.

In Carefree, a woman manifested a US $2 bill, and a man who was about to quit the workshop was visited by a hummingbird he'd meditated on…when it flew into the meeting room right in front of his face. You can bet he stayed for the rest of the weekend after that!

People from all over the world have dimensionalized the funniest things; a fluffy pink key-ring, one red balloon, various animals, feathers, all kinds of toys, and my favorite of all time… porta potties! She'd chosen them because she was fed up with the long lines to the ladies restroom.

* * *

Day one of Carefree was coming to a close, and the five new roomies headed back to our condo to turn in for an early start on Thursday. Here is what I sent via email after the workshop:

> *Hi, Dr. Joe (and the rest of you wonderful people),*
>
> *I gather the standard opening line is "you're not going to believe this but." However, I know you will believe it and even better, it doesn't matter to me whether you do or not.*
>
> *First, get used to hearing from me because I had the most*

miraculous, poignant, loving, fun, delightful, outstanding, transformational time in Carefree.

I realize as I write this on the plane home on Tuesday that I came in with a very big, very powerful desire to become supernatural. I wasn't there to manifest a car, although I truly understand that a car is miraculous for many people. I leave behind judgment, I leave with acceptance.

So, Dr. Joe, you told me to choose a superpower, and I did. The fact that I was too scared to finish my Mind Movie until Wednesday night is no longer relevant. I did it. I went larger than life and that is what I got. Multiplied by 10,000.

Going that big made all the small things along the way unbelievably easy.

On Wednesday evening, you talked about a meditation to teach us how to manifest something physical. I immediately thought of a blue dragon egg that was all lit up inside. Then you said it should be an everyday object, so I scaled back to an egg, a brown one.

Later that evening, I walked into the kitchen at our condo, where five of us were staying. I was the last one up, turning lights off in the kitchen and on the counter was an egg, brown, of course. I picked it up, examined it and thought why is there a random egg sitting on our counter? It wasn't mine so I put it back on the counter and went to bed.

I woke up at 3:40 am laughing. I'd already manifested my object, and we hadn't even started the workshop yet!

Got up, grabbed a magazine that was lying around, and immediately saw an advertisement on the back cover. It had a full-page photo of one brown egg in a single section of a bright blue egg carton.

I was so excited I wanted to go jump-up-and-down on the beds of my roommates and say, "wake up, wake up." I didn't know them very well at the time, but I would totally do that now!

Wow, the fun we had. The amount of falling over, laughing until we cried and rolled on the ground completely restored our souls.

Who Am I Now?

A person who loves to play in creation. There is this dance between intention and allowing that is almost whimsical. When people really want to get good at something, sometimes the dance steps are easy, and sometimes we feel like we have two left feet. Dancing alone often seems more comfortable.

At some point, though, we want to dance with others. Simply because the joy of co-creating is exhilarating! Sharing who we are, what we know and asking for help with what we don't know, satisfies our desire for deep connections.

The more I practice, the more I study the nuances of creation, the more I play with the universe, the more surprises show up in my life.

If you want more manifestations, appreciate every single small thing along the way!

Leanne, one of the fab five roomies, will tell you the dragon's egg became a multi-year quest. I had so much fun with dragons and dragon eggs along the way, I'd stopped even thinking about something physical arriving. Arrive it did, though, exactly as Dr. Joe promised. Wholly unexpected and from someone who didn't know the original story.

* * *

IS THAT AN EGG? - WEDNESDAY, APRIL 29TH

When my son, Connor, gave me my gift on Christmas Day 2017, I almost fainted.

Connor arrived on this planet in a ray of golden light. He sees much and had shut that down, going into a darkness we feared he might not return from. When he's on, which he is these days, he's an effortless manifestor, always teaching me to expect more and allow for easy. His eyes are kind, and his heart is pure. Someday he will stand on a stage and wow the world with his stream of pure, unedited, unapologetic truth.

Out holiday shopping, Connor had gone into a store to get something he had in mind for me. Then the salesperson pointed out hand blown glass dragon's eggs. Each one is unique.

The one he chose for me?

Light blue glass looking into a blue and white spiral ascending upward on the inside.

When I opened the box, I was totally overcome with emotion. It wasn't just the egg, it was knowing the deep connection with my son was now fully restored.

The first thing my excited, gorgeous son showed me once I took it out of the box?

How to hold it up to the light so I could see how it lit up inside.

8

Observer - Thursday, April 30th

It's fun to be the true observer. I never realized how much we operate from our limited perspective, only see through our eyes, perceive with a narrow lens. The world is very different when you expand your view.
   Journal Entry May 20, 2015

To See Without Being Seen

Despite being egged on by the excitement of my early start, the first full day of the Carefree workshop was challenging. One of the things I appreciate about attending a Dr. Joe workshop is the way we get seated. No lining up early, saving places, or elbowing to sit in the front. Upon arrival each day, you reach deep into what I lovingly call the Sorting Hat (from Harry Potter) and pull out a disc with your word for the day. By the end of each workshop, your disc collection is an incredibly accurate keepsake of your journey.

OBSERVER - THURSDAY, APRIL 30TH

It's a pure delight to stand in line and savor the anticipation of reaching into the bag to allow a disc to land in my hand. Then it's the thrill of discovering where I will sit that day and who I will share the word with. The people at the door with the bags share your excitement with a ready hug. No matter what my opinion might be when I draw the disc, my word for each day is always exactly what I need for an opening to new truth and deeper levels of understanding.

* * *

On Thursday, April 30th, I pulled **Observer** from the hat. Perplexing?!

* * *

In every workshop, Dr. Joe teaches for a while, then he'll have you *"turn to the person next to you and explain"* what you just heard to reinforce the material. Then we apply what we've learned in a meditation, take a break, come back, dance for a few songs for fun and do it all again.

Dr. Joe's website says; *"Through his advanced workshops around the world, he has performed extensive research on the effects of meditation, including epigenetic testing, brain mapping, and individual energy field testing and has amassed scientific evidence of amazing healings – by participants who have learned his model of personal transformation."*

It was the scientific information that initially attracted me to Dr. Joe's work, so I was thrilled to be part of this extensive research project. Each willing participant was randomly assigned to a scientific test. My contribution was the opportunity to be brain mapped during a meditation.

Others, including Bradley, wore monitoring devices from the Heart Math Institute[12] for 24 hours. At the start of each meditation, Dr. Joe asked us to send love to them. Later we were told that the device readings showed that the entire group went into heart/brain coherence at the exact same moment when we were sending them the love!

I tried so hard that first day, but mostly I wanted to feel love. I tried not to be a taker, but I found it hard to give what I didn't have.

* * *

I spent a lot of time in the first couple of days attempting to control my environment. This was to be the last event at the Carefree Resort as Dr. Joe's work was becoming increasingly popular, and space there was maxed out. As it was, over 500 people were in the room, and to me, it felt like we were on top of each other. I'd had claustrophobia for years and have had panic attacks, complete with hyperventilation while trying to navigate large stores or shopping malls.

We were sitting at round tables of ten people, and I wanted to be able to lie down during that portion of a meditation and have no one touch me. I wanted to be far enough away that anyone coughing or snoring would not annoy me. I wanted a quick route to the restroom because I was anxious about being able to empty my bladder before each meditation. I was always cold from blown-out adrenals, so I had a bag with socks and blankets and layers so I would be warm enough.

In Dr. Joe's language, my body and my programs were controlling me, and I was willingly, yet unconsciously, honoring those programs!

Stress limits your ability to see possibilities.

It didn't occur to me that I could move my chair away from the table and set up against a wall.

> *May 13, 2015-Journal Entry*
>
> *I feel like everything I've ever wished for, wanted, or longed for is now with me, around me, happening to me.*
>
> *My relationship with my mother is pristine, delicious, and divine. My Dad just told me, "I love you too!" He never does that.*
>
> *I can barely keep track of the moments of wonder, the changes in my relationships, the changes in me. I don't know how I created this. I only know I am grateful beyond measure. I knew I had power, but wow-I have POWER x 16,000.*
>
> *My relationship with my mother is pristine, delicious, and divine. My Dad just told me, "I love you too!" He never does that.*
>
> *Always the right page, always the right timing. I stop writing minutes before someone wakes up, comes home, or calls. I don't fight it. I just do it.*

Grace is an interesting place. It is so soft, so beautiful, so accepting.

It's been 18 or 19 years since I revealed my Functional Identity – Gracious Guide. I still have the paper, decorated with stickers. (This was a session done for me by a gifted holistic practitioner in 1997. My Mind Movies end with "I am the Gracious Guide")

For many of those years, I didn't even think of this paper, much less believe I could ever embody what was written upon it. Years of children growing up, relationships, some good, some very, very hard.

I understand something important now. I have always believed ALL things are possible. The fact that I didn't know how, or what, or when, never meant the impossible. At the core of my being I knew all possibilities existed.

That is one stable foundation in which to enter a Dr. Joe workshop.

The months after the Progressive Workshop were easy, then hard, and then very, very hard.

I threw all my faith into Carefree. I went knowing I would die in some way. Mostly because I knew I could not live with myself the way I was and ever be happy enough to remain on earth.

I arrived in Arizona with a stone in my heart that none of my many tools could dislodge.

* * *

It's almost impossible to recall the version of me who attended a large meeting in Toronto a month before Carefree. I was sitting with my team, beside a very close friend. We were shown a YouTube video of an Olympic athlete named Derek Redmond, who was favored to win the 400-meter race in Barcelona in 1992[13]. Set to Josh Groban's, *You Raise Me Up,* the video is a heart-wrenching journey of watching Derek fall, then struggle to get up and decide to continue. Derek's father jumps onto the track and walks his limping son around the track, finally releasing him to hobble over the finish line on his own. 65,000 people in the stands are moved beyond tears, and the applause is thunderous.

Sobs overtook my body as I watched, but not as much for him. I was crying because I wondered, *"Who would pick me up when I stumbled? Who would walk me to the finish line?"*

There I was, surrounded by people who loved and respected me, receiving success and recognition in my business, able to drive home to my family in my free car, yet I completely broke down because I felt so alone, so miserable with the choices I'd made that left me disconnected from the many, many people who love me.

OBSERVER - THURSDAY, APRIL 30TH

Their love cannot touch you if you do not love yourself.

Nothing much touched me in the days leading into Carefree. Apart from a breakdown, I quickly attempted to hide during that meeting, I could not be emotionally moved. Not music, not hugs, not sessions done for others, or sessions received.

There was no placebo for that heart of stone.

* * *

Two months later, I was sitting at the Observer table - watching everyone to make sure I was going to get what I needed to feel safe, holding my emotions in check, mind tuned to the Endless Chatter Channel.

"Was I going to get a good seat?
Who would I sit beside?
Would it be close to the exit?
Would I get a good view of the stage?
Were people sharing the learning, or rambling on about themselves?
Did I have enough clothes to stay warm?
Who danced during the breaks, and who didn't?"

This was my unconscious ingrained habit. Always on guard, assessing the lay of the land, my brain endlessly plotting to maintain order around me.

I relaxed a bit during Thursday morning, slowly surrendering control. I hadn't stepped in yet.

> *May 6, 2015-Journal Entry*
> *The part where we lie down was a mass of bodies. I pretzelled my way onto the floor, trying not to touch anyone. I met a lovely lady who graciously bonded our arms. We had no choice-we were*

> that tight in the middle of the room.
> I learned to adjust, I learned to relax without perfect conditions. I allowed human encounters. It was nice.

Late that afternoon, the person sitting beside me that I'd been sharing with all day, altered my perception of Observer.

> **"The true Observer sees all, with truth and compassion," she told me. AHA. I wasn't observing to be able to control my environment. I was to rise above, to become the observer of humanity, earth, and its inhabitants with patience and absolutely no judgment.**

Who Am I Now?

I took myself to Ikea in the fall of 2016, easily navigated the store, asked for help to find something, checked out, found a nice young man to watch my stuff so I could get the car, then he kindly helped me load it up.

> **It sounds like a completely normal, rather dull, shopping experience, right?**

It wasn't until the drive home that it hit me... Ikea used to totally freak me out! In years past, I would have staggered through clutching my big yellow bag, overwhelmed by the lack of escape routes, close to tears. I'd either buy too much or forget what I'd come for.

For years I would carefully shop the perimeters of large stores, dreading the claustrophobia and wondering if today would turn into an anxiety attack.

I'd learned to manage it by planning out my shopping routes, going to the same stores over and over because I'd be familiar with the layout. I could last about an hour in a mall before needing to stop and eat.

That day at Ikea, without even knowing it, I'd mastered my nemesis and was driving away happily eating a $1 double twist ice cream cone!

* * *

These are the side effects of doing **The Work**, as Dr. Joe calls it. So many things resolve themselves. And they are so GONE, we don't even notice their absence.

I didn't know it at the time, but sitting at the Observer table on Day One allowed me to begin to let go of being hyper-vigilant.

I was able to see from a different vantage point, and no longer had the need to evaluate everything around me as a potential threat. By moving to a place of compassion for myself I was able to stay in the room for a special Native American ceremony later that evening. In the past, drumming had caused me such emotional distress I'd have to leave.

Many others, including my roommates, Jeannie and Leanne, were enthralled by the drumming. Perhaps I was missing something? It obviously meant a lot to Dr. Joe that this tribe had agreed to share their sacred ceremony with us.

Initially, I chose to stay because I didn't want to dishonor anyone by leaving. Although I was uncomfortable at first, I was able to see my ingrained response was associated with a program associated with the old me.

> *This is called awareness; when we can see our behavior as something separate from the person we really are. Then we can make a choice to have a new response, a response that allows more joy, more peace, and more fulfillment.*

I decided to see drumming from a different vantage point and be open to something new. The result? I overcame myself and enjoyed the evening.

* * *

Those small shifts in perspective from my day at the Observer table were new choices I'd made to invite people in. Like not moving away from a person touching me during the meditation, gently encouraging my fellow Observers to dance, staying in the room to experience the drumming.

Each of those choices began opening the door to my heart, allowing a little more light into each crack of least resistance.

I was starting to feel safe here on this planet.

9

Grace - Friday, May 1, 2015

When we see someone as whole, complete, and perfect, when we see their soul, what is in their heavily guarded heart, we allow them a chance, if only for a moment, to see it for themselves.
Journal Entry June 9, 2015

My memory of this day is still crystal clear. I was to be brain mapped for the 6 am meditation and had to arrive even earlier to get prepped.

I burst into tears when I drew the disc for my table. Day Two: Grace. This state of being and all it means is interwoven into the fabric of my life. It's in all of my Mind Movies and is inscribed on my wedding band three times.

The Grace table was located at the very back of the room, right by the door. Go me! My intention from Thursday resulted in more than enough space for me to lie down and get out of the room quickly, but I was still running the joke of me being "the back of the bus girl."

Turned out, the technician for the electroencephalography (EEG) was from the Toronto area. We got to know each other as she put the very tight cap on my head, and poured the goo in the holes so she could attach the electrodes to my scalp. An EEG records the electrical activity of the brain, and I was thrilled to know my data would be part of an extensive scientific study.

Many people think the wires go into your skull. They do not! Nothing about being brain mapped hurts, but you do end up with a freaky Halloween worthy hairdo. I was pretty happy the early start meant I got time for a shower over the breakfast break.

* * *

Dr. Joe taught the *Blessing of the Energy Centers*[14] meditation and introduced me to choosing symbols for each center. Anxiety was building in me during the explanation. Back then, I was very conscious of whether I could hold my urine for an extended meditation. I couldn't make a last-minute run to the bathroom because I was tethered to the machine by the cap.

We spent some time writing down our symbols, then the technician did a baseline of my brain at rest, noted that I was a bit nervous, and the meditation began.

Three months later, I received a report of my brain map. The results showed quick entry into a meditative state, rapid connection to the field, and strong visualizations throughout. Close to the end of the EEG when the meditation was almost over, the screen activity started to go crazy, and my entire brain lit up.

* * *

As the meditation was winding down, people were lying down on the floor with soft music playing. I was permitted to put my head on a table and put my arms and hands beside my head.

Not content to simply do nothing, I decided to check in energetically on my daughter, my son, and the friend I'd brought with me in spirit.

Out of nowhere, a clear female voice spoke to me. The voice sounded very familiar.

These were not thoughts I was having, this was a voice I was hearing.

The words she spoke are as clear to me today as the moment I heard them for the first time. Her words were straightforward and filled with gentle love. I was being bathed in grace.

"Dwyn, everyone is safe. You are safe, everyone in your world is safe."

The voice continued, *"You don't have to take care of anyone anymore. Everyone is exactly where they're supposed to be."*

To my utter surprise, she then said, *"Dwyn, you are officially off duty. You can go play now. Go, play!"*

By now, the realization of my experience was being processed in my brain. Intense emotions had overtaken my body, and I was crying with astonishment and joy. My body was shaking uncontrollably, and my right hand started moving up from the table on its own volition.

I was vaguely aware of my hand lifting, probably 8"-10" off the table, and it was vibrating with an immense amount of energy.

Once the voice told me to go play, I left my body in an instant and started flying around the top of the room!

I was free.

I was so light and joyous and happy. I was this little kid who'd been dismissed from a lifetime of timeouts in a corner, flying around for the thrill of it, experiencing my first taste of true freedom.

* * *

I hadn't connected a condition known as hyper-vigilance to my lifelong tendency to scan my environment to assess whether I was safe. My mother had always been emotionally unpredictable. From the time I was a little girl, I'd learned to observe my surroundings so I could predict, and evade, what she might do next. She called me sneaky; I now know I was adapting my behavior so I could survive in a hostile environment. I carried this low-level hum of feeling unsafe into adulthood.

All my years of therapy and inner work had never brought hyper-vigilance into view.

After the meditation, I was giddy with glee. Childlike wonder and exuberance made the world seem new and bright and shiny.

* * *

As always, Bradley came to find me and rounded us up to go back to the condo for breakfast. I was jumping up and down with excitement, goo in my hair, and babbling a mile a minute. Attempting to describe my experience and the pure clarity of her voice.

It took over two years before the source of that voice was finally revealed.

All of my senses were heightened. The sun shining felt like warm embrace, I could see the intricate details of the cactus and the birds. The shower felt like my first encounter with water pouring over my skin. It was sensual, and I remember touching it and tasting it.

The sheer joy of being physical was glorious!

In other news, my right hand had so much energy in it I couldn't bring it down to my side. It was "frozen" in a bit of a wave as if it was still hovering over the table! What's a girl to do?

As Bradley writes in his book, *Decide*, "our hearts will guide us to make decisions if we trust it."

During the walk back to our condo, I'd joked about my right hand. "It has so much energy in it, what am I going to do with it all?" I asked, only to have Bradley jump up and down, saying, "I'll take it, I'll take it!" We stopped, I asked him where he wanted me to place my hand. He said, "my heart." So I did.

We both felt and saw the fireworks! Bolts of lightning came out of my hand into his heart, and we could see these glorious fiery colors. Oranges and reds and yellows and blues. He almost fell over from the power.

I'd learned how to do energy healing back in the mid-'90s but never really used it.

Plus, this was a power I'd never felt before!

* * *

Turns out Bradley's heart really needed that jump-start. He rarely talks about his "voodoo curse diagnosis" or the fact that his Dad was dying of cancer, as the reasons for seeking out Dr. Joe's work. For him, just being in Carefree was a miracle.

Dr. Joe does a monthly Teleclass, where he takes questions and much to Bradley's surprise, his name had been called the prior February. He'd shared a story of meditating in the woods and having a deer walk up and sit down close to him. When he'd connected with the deer and asked for her help, she took his symptoms away for a few days. Bradley wanted to know how to have that happen for him consistently. He also mentioned that he'd love to get to Carefree, but it was sold out. Dr. Joe had his staff call and offer him a spot the very next day.

Honestly, this guy can manifest anything! He's open to trying new things, a sponge for new information, and he lives life with wonder and enthusiasm.

With my inner child now out of her childhood prison, Bradley was the perfect person to show me what being a carefree kid was really like.

> *Adwynna, you put an orange rod in the area of my heart, and I feel it. Thank you. I have my hand on it as I cry and look out the window. It gives me strength and love, and joy. It's a bottomless source of energy.*
>
> Post Workshop Email from Bradley, May 8, 2015

* * *

When I found my friends by the pool Friday evening, they were getting ready to do video testimonials. I recall saying I'd wait until after the workshop as I was dressed to go swimming. Still, Bradley and Jeannie were all in, and the person behind the camera encouraged me to just tell it. I'm so grateful to all of them because I have a permanent record of my breakthrough the day it happened.

You can watch the video on the Dr. Joe Dispenza YouTube channel by searching for "Adwynna" or go to resources.adwynna.com and get the video plus more of this story. I ask a question at the end of the video, *"Who knows what's going to happen next?"*

Get ready for the answer, because that question blew the doors wide open to a weekend beyond belief.

Who Am I Now?

When I watch my video testimonial, I see how lit up I was that May Day in 2015. Seeing it unedited right after, knowing I'd done it entirely off the cuff, I realized I could speak from the heart without any need for a script. For the first time in my life, I saw the inner me reflected back to me; poised, glowing, beautiful, playful, emanating joy and awe.

And I liked her! A lot!

She was my future self, and when she showed up live and in person, she was even more glorious than I'd ever imagined. I've used the clip about being a Light Being in my Mind Movies, and today, I can watch that video and have it completely alter my state.

* * *

Understanding the connection between safety and freedom became part of my mission. I want every person to feel safe to be themselves, to walk this earth, knowing they are always taken care of.

This involved opening to more awareness of what I believed about our choice to live here on earth, my concept of death, and the dance of judgment between opposites. Exploring the deeper purpose of our relationship with light/dark, good/bad, right/wrong, negative/positive.

Although feeling safe to be me happened in Carefree, feeling safe to be me publicly took much longer.

I've had to accept that I talk about things that make some people uncomfortable. Like death. Like choices we make to stay stuck. Like being guided by Light Beings. I used to feel uncomfortable when others were uncomfortable. This is why I didn't tell people my sisters were dead for the longest time, and why it took me so long to share who I am openly.

In 2014 I'd been struck deeply by this quote from *You Are the Placebo*, "*We have to become comfortable with being uncomfortable.*" I know what that means now, in my mind, and in my experience.

> **I left Carefree knowing I was protected and had always been, even as a helpless child. I met the Light Beings who walk with me, offer me guidance, and answer my endless questions.**

* * *

There is a reason we are told to put safety first. Yet feeling safe isn't attained by walking around the planet trying to avoid all the things, people, and experiences that could hurt us.

Safety is knowing in every cell of our bodies that we are all, as the voice in Carefree told me, "*always safe.*"

When my kids were little, I read a parenting book that explained why having a routine for them would help them feel safe enough in their world to explore outside of that safe place. Kids who had a foundation of love, who knew they would get fed at the same time each day, that someone would always be there when they cried. Those were the kids willing to take more risks, be more adventurous, and openly ask questions.

In contrast, my childhood taught me it was safer to live my life according to the rules of my mother, even though those rules were a constantly moving target. Ways to win my mother's love often changed from day-to-day and sometimes from hour-to-hour. In my quest to become a good girl, with no real understanding of what that meant, I wandered lost for a long, long time.

Knowing I was safe finally freed me to be me. Even though I annoyed some people with my youthful exuberance, I stayed with this journey of discovery.

I've had more and more mystical experiences, and more and more of my questions are being answered all the time.

> ***It became my deepest desire to discover how to help others find that feeling of safety, to have that knowing of being taken care of, to revel in the bliss of that freedom.***

* * *

Results of the May 1, 2015 Brain Map

The scientific testing at Dr. Joe workshops is conducted by a research team. We were permitted to purchase an explanation of our individual brain map results, so I said yes to my report and a 30-minute consultation with Dr. Jeffrey Fannin[15]. Dr. Fannin is a neuroscientist and one of the world's top brain experts, and he led the scientific team in Carefree.

My consultation took place about four months after the EEG. Dr. Fannin was very interested in my mystical experience as it helps to interpret the results of the scans.

Having a renowned scientist explain to me what went on in my brain during a breakthrough of that magnitude has been an incredible gift. Remember, I'd learned to meditate in 1996 then done it off and on for a few years, starting again in November 2014 at the Progressive Workshop. That's over a decade of rarely, if ever, meditating. Even in the weeks coming into Carefree, I'd become very intermittent.

Something compelling happens when you have external scientific validation of a breakthrough experience that is so challenging to describe. First, it feels really, really good and mostly it makes you want to do more of it!

This is what Dr. Fannin said to wrap up our time together:

> "You have all of the markers of an advanced meditator; strong connection to the field, strong gateway to your subconscious, the markers at Alpha that let you be present, the area that shows you have very, very strong visualizations.
>
> "By the end of the meditation, you are in the zone. A hyper-coherent state with lots of information being processed with very strong emotions. Your ability to free yourself is rare. We do not see that very often, and we've seen hundreds of scans over the past 1 1/2 years. By the end, you are in the upper frequencies and are just all in on the experience."
>
> "Learning to let go and allow is one of the hardest things people have to do in these meditations, and scientifically, you are doing it all exactly right."

To see more from the Brain Map Report go to resources.adwynna.com

10

Focus- Saturday, May 2, 2015

The debt of gratitude we all should have to our stress, anxiety, illnesses, traumas, and tragedies is enormous. Without them, we would never have found that tiny piece of fairy dust to grasp onto and follow our way home.
Journal Entry May 31, 2015

By Saturday, I had so much energy the 6 am start didn't faze me at all. When I pulled my disc for the day, I was not surprised that my word was Focus, nor was I shocked to discover my table was, once again, at the very back of the room! The good news? I had tons of room to lie down directly in front of the brain map tables.

Then and there, I decided to let go of my back-of-the-bus belief and set an intention to be closer to the front on Sunday.

The meditation we did before breakfast was the turning point for the entire group. There are two things I recall clearly. First, during the breathing technique, energy hit my brain and body like never before.

I was determined to use "The Breath" to break free from my past, and when the energy kept moving up and into my brain, my body was releasing so much trapped energy I was shaking uncontrollably, sweating profusely and loud sounds were emitting from my being in a voice I would never use in my daily life.

I was vaguely aware I could stop it and also vaguely aware that I didn't want to.

So I'm guessing right about now you might be wondering why anyone would use their time and money to travel to a workshop with hundreds of people to flail around like the girl in The Exorcist? Although I do lovingly call it *The Damn Breath,* I know without any doubt it's the secret sauce in the pasta dish of *The Work* that results in thousands of profound healings and rapid breakthroughs.

My brain mapping tech from Friday commented later that she'd seen me in the throes of really letting go. She didn't look at me like I had horns growing out of my head, so I took that to be a good thing.

Towards the end of that meditation, when we were all lying down on the floor, someone started to laugh.

I've had that happen to me a few times post-meditation, so I completely understand how a case of the giggles can engulf you. The laughter caught fire, and the entire room erupted. People would laugh until they ran out of breath, there would be a few seconds of calm, and then it would start again.

Imagine a room of 500+ people howling with laughter, tears streaming, gasping for air, rolling around on the floor, grabbing their stomachs.

It was the best purge EVER!

When it finally ceased, and Dr. Joe brought us back to the room, with much hugging and more laughing. People went to breakfast with huge smiles on their faces, chatting away to each other. The energy had shifted, and we were finally a cohesive group.

Now we could go to the next level.

*　*　*

The rest of Saturday consisted of meditations with our Mind Movies and another out of body experience for me deep into the faerie realm where I was greeted as the Queen of the Faeries. When I came back from the realm, I was flitting around the top of the room, still deep in meditation, sprinkling faerie dust on the people below.

I pay close attention when something that happens in my inner world is validated by something that happens in my outer world.

When the meditation was over, I was lying on the floor and looked up to see a man with big blue eyes offering his hand to help me up. He took my hand like he was helping a queen into a carriage. His words to me as I gratefully stood up?

"Greetings, M'lady."

Who Am I Now?

The man who helped me to my feet in regal fashion has become a most divine friend. He and I kept showing up at the same Dr. Joe events where we'd engage in deep and unusual conversations. Turns out, he's very accustomed to traveling the higher realms and had actually seen me flitting around the room as my fairy self during the Saturday meditation.

Two years later, I discovered he'd had what he called a Kundalini Awakening about ten years prior. It was as unexpected for him as my spiritual awakening had been for me. I'd started writing this book by the time we had our discussion, so I was thrilled to compare notes with someone who'd had a similar experience.

He reminded me recently that my childlike, playful energy was what drew him to me in Carefree. He'd observed me as I Awakened and often sought me out because he found my curious and light-hearted presence uplifting and fascinating.

Perhaps he'd seen himself from ten years ago in me?

This man has helped me access higher levels and bypass some of the stigma associated with mystical experiences. We've also shared a full moon night after a Dr. Joe event that was intermingled with altered states, lucid dreams, and mutual astral travel. No plant medicine or mind-altering substances required! Thankfully, we have a witness to our trippy night! Plus, I recorded a recap and a deep dive conversation with him about what it means to have a spiritual awakening. Just so we'd have it "on the record."

* * *

The future I thought I was creating when I did my Mind Movie for Carefree did not include experiences like the ones I had with this friend. Those were beyond my wildest imaginings at that time. Yet, when I watch that movie now I totally see how I opened myself to the mystical!

If you are curious, you can listen to my conversation with him about Spiritual Awakenings, or watch my 2015 Mind Movie resources.adwynna.com

The Mind Movie music I used was composed for me by Craig Young, who you will meet in the chapter called *The Song of Your Soul*. At the time, the composition was called *Dragons Rising*. Craig has since remixed it in 432 hertz and released it as *Rise of the Dragons*. The song is now used for the breathing technique at Dr. Joe Workshops.

This means that when I do *The Damn Breath* my body has a deep visceral response to that music, taking me to even more magical, mystical places.

Such is the power of music to free us into the unknown.

11

Miraculous - Sunday, May 3, 2015

Every day I live in grace and wonder. It's almost impossible to record all the miracles that happen from moment to moment.

Darkness Cannot Survive Long in the Light

As I discovered, Dr. Joe's meditations are long and start very early. I certainly thought the staff was nuts asking me to show up to be brain mapped for 5:30 am and figured I'd be there with the other unlucky few who'd drawn the short straw for the scientific testing. I didn't know *everyone* shows up for 6 am and that by the time Sunday rolled around, I'd be wide awake and happy to be walking in the moonlight at 3:30 am to get there.

Not only did I get through a four-hour meditation a mere five days later after wondering how I'd get up for 6 am, but I also emerged from it transformed, having experienced a rebirth so profound I could neither walk steadily nor speak.

Here is an email I sent to Dr. Joe about a month later. It references a few things about the room setup and the meditation that require advance clarification:

1. Everyone agrees to stay in the room for the entire meditation.
2. Dr. Joe has us sit up and lie down at various points.
3. There are ten people at a round table, each with a chair and space behind the chair to lie down.
4. Some people leave their table and set up yoga mats, blankets, pillows, etc. along the walls or in front of the stage, so they have extra space.
5. A hula hoop was hanging from the ceiling as a metaphor for an interdimensional portal.[16]

Dear Dr. Joe,

28 days from Carefree Friday. The day my life began its dramatic change. Every day I live in grace and wonder. It's now almost impossible to record all the miracles that happen from moment to moment.

I listened to your May 28 Teleclass and gained an even deeper understanding and was reminded to dig deeper to ferret out those icky pieces still stuck inside my body. The result was a meditation that took me inside my heart, and then body, to uproot some hugely stuck, <u>very</u> difficult to move pieces. Because of the complete trust I have in this process, I was able, with <u>much</u> divine assistance, to dig, pull, shine a light on this junk and get it gone. My body this morning feels it too. I allow for integration, will walk my dog, and restore myself.

I sat down to write about the Sunday 4 AM meditation because at the end of it (you will recall some people were laughing), the choices I made truly changed me.

We walked from our condo to the resort at 3:30 AM under the full moon with gathering cloud setting the mood. Jeannie was behind, and my other roomies had gone ahead. Bradley just in front of me.

I felt he wanted me to hold his hand, so I caught up, slipped my right hand into his left. He closed his fingers on mine and said, "I really wanted you to hold my hand," I said, "I know." We walked together in silence and awe. I was aware of Jeannie and motioned to her to catch up and hold my other hand.

When we got into the event room, I got my wish!

After 4 days, I'd finally scored a table near the front of the room at the side. I'd have lots of space to lie down and be able to see you clearly on stage!

When I saw that the table name was Miraculous, I cried. Those table names are pure super genius!

A man with the same name of my ex-boyfriend was beside me. We said hello, he said his name, I said: "of course." To my left was a woman who looked familiar. We'd met at the Progressive. She reminded me of my ex-business partner and mentor.

So there I am sitting between the two biggest heartbreaks in my life, at the Miraculous table!

This was going to be interesting.

The meditation begins, the energy is epic. I am ready. Breath, music, the sound of your voice. At varying points, I went into the void. Crossed into it with a distinct physical feeling of going. It sounded like a click, and then I'm looking around with my eyes wide open under my eye mask. Or not, I can't really tell if my eyes are open or closed. No matter. I'm gazing at all the blackness all around me, I am aware my head is moving.

On one of the lying down parts, various Light Beings arrive to work on my body, stretching out joints, aligning my pelvis, doing surgery on my midsection. I can feel the adjustments and my body moving on its own. Am occasionally uncomfortable, although not in pain.

My Dragons breathe life force into my crown and into my body. At one point, my heart is so wide open and enormous that I gather everyone in the room and allow them to flow through my heart, entering from the back and exiting out of the front in a supernatural conga line.

I'm totally out of body by now. Flying, visiting people, aware of other

MIRACULOUS - SUNDAY, MAY 3, 2015

Beings and Guides. It's all pretty flowy and awesome.

And then it isn't.

Lying down, I've become aware that someone is making a run for the side door, which is right beside me. They are panicky and pushing on it to get out. They're not supposed to leave the meditation. It's the agreement we all made. Light floods our space. I'm jolted out of my happy place.

Attempt to settle. Lying down again, I'm aware that someone is now regularly kicking my foot. " I'm holding onto my space" and not moving. Bruce nudges me. A person beside me is snoring; I'm convinced it's the woman who reminded my of my ex-mentor. She is occasionally making gagging sounds, which I'm hoping means she will stop snoring.

Bliss left the building with the escapee. I am now frustrated.

I break the "rules" and lift my mask, only to encounter the rear end of a woman who has decided to do yoga against the wall rather than lie down.

Her movements were leading her to kick me occasionally. So now, I'm not floating in the void. I'm on the ground, and I am grumpy!

One of my roommates had suggested that when things like this happen, I should send healing love and light to calm everyone down. Not working!!!

And then I get it. In a wave of realization, I understand that I am not responsible for anyone else's experience but my own.

If they want to sleep, snore, leave, scream, cry, do the downward dog or cuddle the person next to them, that is their choice.

They have not asked me for help; they haven't asked me for light or love. Who am I to impose what I believe they need? Who am I to interfere with their experience?

Right then, right now, I want to get to that portal. It doesn't matter if I have to shift my position, it doesn't matter what I have to do, I'm getting myself through it. (Which was my level of understanding of how a portal worked at the time)

I gathered myself and my belongings up. I got between my chair legs with my head all the way under the table, tucked in as far as I could go. I pulled my knees onto my chest, covered my ears with my hands to block it all out.

Then I gathered all the pieces inside of me that I could find and told them I was going through that portal, and they were welcome to come with me, or they could stay behind. If they stayed behind, they were leaving my body.

It was <u>their</u> choice, but my choice was the freedom I knew was through the hula hoop hanging from the ceiling.

We got up to do the last part of the meditation, and I'm sitting in my chair. It was wonderful.

We lay back down. Suddenly, I had plenty of space on the floor. I was peaceful, and my body felt terrific. I was light and in love, and ripples of gratitude were sweeping through me. I was in the meditation and aware of how great I felt in my body lying there on the floor.

And then someone laughed.

It was the wrong laugh, not a sincere heartfelt laugh. Yet some people caught onto it, and minor waves would sprinkle through the assembled group. I was aware that some people were upset, annoyed, or joining in the laughing. I briefly thought of the day before when the room had exploded with joy and recalled the video of the subway and how laughter was contagious. This was different, and I didn't want to get swept up in that contagion.

Dr. Joe, I made a choice to stay in my state. I chose my peace, love, and light. I decided to stay in gratitude. I observed others but did not decide to join them. I allowed them to have whatever experience they wanted to create.

That was my most significant gift from Carefree. The ability to choose my experience and allow others to choose theirs.

Now I am very different with people. I see their pain, and I stand in my grace to allow them to step into that space. Most of the time, they move in, become calm, focused, and clear.

I've done nothing, absolutely nothing, but see them for who they really are in their heart and allow them to step into that light.

To say this has altered my relationships is an understatement. The change in my client sessions is profound. Sessions are focused, shorter in time, which I have long wanted. They get more in less time and feel totally satisfied. They want to pay me more, for there is no amount of money to compensate for what they just received.

But it's the daily interactions I enjoy the most. Deep connection to everyone I encounter: human, animal, bird, fish, insects, trees, plants - doesn't matter.

It's all holy-each a sacred encounter.

All of this and more happened during my first ever four-hour meditation. When it ended, I had no idea how much time had passed. I could not talk. There were no words. I could barely walk; I felt like I had new legs that didn't work very well yet. I was freezing and somewhat dazed.

Bradley found me in the crowd and was chatting away to other people. I let him know I needed to go outside and warm up. He told me not to leave without him, so I went out into the warm sunny morning and sat on a wall, soaking in the desert heat, trying to get some feeling in my legs.

Oddly, I felt empty. A peaceful empty though, like my previous life had poured out of me, and I was freshly born.

Who Am I Now?

I refer to May 3, 2015, as my B'Earthday. The day I was reborn into a new body and a new reality. Attempting to recount a four-hour vivid meditation and add some perspective is a challenging task. Things that happened in a few minutes take much longer to describe.

People who have these re-birth experiences struggle to find words to convey the depth of emotion. When we say the word love, we may describe the sensation of being wrapped in a warm blanket of bliss. We know we aren't only connected to all that is, we ARE all that is! Mostly though, people report that they feel like they are home.

Home is a massive word. It evokes feelings of safety and belonging. Of abiding love and connection. Of being accepted for who we are, knowing our place in the vast expanse of the universe. For me, May 3, 2015, was the day I found Home. Right there in my heart, where it had always been.

> May 15, 2015-*Journal Entry*
>
> *Darkness cannot survive long in the light.*
>
> *As I write this, dawn is here. The light is grey and flat. The sun is rising behind the sky, starting its ascent into another day.*
>
> *As it rises, the dark edges and cool grays will fade, allowing light into its prisms and creating a whole new day.*
>
> *This is happening for me. As I allow the pure, strong light of love into my being, it is moving out those grays. The drab colors I used to wear, replaced by pinks and blues, yellows, and greens.*
>
> *I like the feeling of light. I walk taller, softer, ever so soft on the ground. It's as if my feet move on air and not on the previously solid matter I once believed was the earth.*
>
> *The light of love, the one you so graciously allowed me to discover as it was birthed - all fresh and new from from its previously frozen state. You held me in my most vulnerable moment, re-birth, allowing me to silently become the new me.*
>
> *That foundation of pure love was an entirely new experience, one I was deprived of at my physical birth when I was whisked away from my mother and put into a nursery, finally given to her five days later, only to be greeted with outright revulsion.*
>
> *A proper foundation creates a solid structure, and with love as*

the foundation, safety is built into its moorings. There is enough play in the pillars set solidly into the ground to allow for movement and growth, not to mention the occasional gale force wind and screaming hurricane of rage, wrath and fury. All of this and more is now departing as light enters my being, burning through old patterns, beliefs and fears.

All is new, fresh, and I am alive with wonder. There is a stillness inside me and my transformation is so complete I cannot even recall the feeling of the continuous low-level hum of anxiety that defined my prior daily existence.

12

Joyous Beyond Condition

I've just written for ages. Less frenzy, more flow. Gorgeous words pouring out of my pen. It feels good, it feels connected. I love me when I'm writing.
  Actually, I love me all the time now.
  Journal Entry May 27, 2015

Bradley said goodbye to us after dinner on Sunday at the same Mexican restaurant where we'd all gotten to know each the previous Wednesday. The day I'd looked at him and said, "you will be the person who gets me to write!"

He and I stood on the sidewalk, looking at the full moon we'd walked under at 3:30 am. It felt like hundreds of lifetimes ago. We didn't talk on that sidewalk, we didn't need to. It was pretty clear our friendship was just getting started.

The sky was starting to light up as a desert storm moved in. I'd never witnessed the moon fully visible on one part of the horizon, while crazy bolts of lightning danced across the other side of the sky. I kept filling my lungs with this intoxicating ozone created by the storm. Despite the long day, I stayed up for hours watching it play across the landscape from the balcony of our condo, finally getting to know Leanne.

* * *

Bradley wrote this after the workshop and posted it to the Dr. Joe Forum.

> *Dearest forum friends: this is a note to myself and to others to help them see that we can get beyond our condition. I remember Dr. Joe talking about it in a teleclass, and I thought this whole "beyond your condition" stuff was just a bunch of hype. "Yay! Let's just be happy! Forget your condition! Once you get beyond it, it will disappear!" Blah blah blah. Gag! Blech. Uh-huh, whatever. But this weekend changed all that.*
>
> **You can get beyond your condition. But then what?**
>
> *Dr. Joe talks about the point where you are so _____ (fill in your blank: joyous, happy, grateful, all of the above) that you no longer care if you have your condition. That's what he's seen in his testimonials and case studies. I've never been able to grasp that as the condition in my mind was so great, so huge, so momentous that I couldn't imagine anything being greater than it. Until now.*
>
> *But wait a sec. The disease or condition is everything! It's at least a part of you, right? A big part, no, a huge part! No, it's who you are! Don't you dare pretend it's not. Now then, glad we got that sorted.*

CAREFREE, IT STARTS WITH OPEN

When you're so deep in your condition or state or issues, it's hard (read: seemingly impossible) to imagine a life beyond it, much less joy or anything positive.

But the joy I felt this past weekend at the workshop in Carefree was so overwhelming, it overtook my entire self. As if it's a bike race and the condition has been out front. If you know your bike racing, it was even out in the lead pack, broken away from the main pack (called the peloton). But I've caught up with it this weekend and even surpassed it. I'm not sure I've broken away from the peloton just yet, but we're out there in front and have the wind at our backs.

Sorry, quick editor's note: I just realized that I subconsciously switched from "I" to "we" in the previous sentence. This weekend in Carefree has truly changed my "team" from being the trio of "me, myself and I" to a force of new friends, new information and new understanding. Whoa. Unexpected.

We've also seen the front, we know we can be out there, so we've had that glorious taste of victory, of being in front. We have the wind in our hair, the bugs in our teeth, and we're smiling as our legs just pump us forward effortlessly. We're in such good shape, the spinning of our legs doesn't cause us fatigue; it's like walking or breathing: we just do it, and we move forward.

I cried buckets this past weekend. *Uncontrollable sobbing the likes I'm not sure I've ever had. No, ever ever. What emotions are escaping me? In my head, that physical skull, I feel a bursting energy, but it's not sadness. Somehow it's joy and gratitude and love. Mostly love. So why the crying? There is also sadness. Maybe*

I'm just stirring up all kinds of dust in there, and it's letting out what's been packed down after years of trampling. But the joy I felt at the end of the workshop and then in the airport and finally again in the cancer hospital with my parents was so strong that it overpowered my condition.

I could honestly say (and in fact, did say to myself, aloud even) that I was so joyous, so full of love and gratitude that those emotions were stronger than the emotions that I felt towards my physical condition. I didn't think I'd ever get there. I wasn't sure if it was even possible.

Now that we've experienced it, we know it's possible to go there. We understand it better, we've been there. So even if we fall back into the peloton and it again takes the lead, we know we can get out in front again. Maybe as we pass it, this time we'll stick a bike pump into their spokes ... buy hey, no hard feelings, really, right?

If I could murder my condition, would I?

Do I want to see this condition tumbling through the air and bloodied and bruised? Well, yes. Do I want to see it dead? As I wrote those words, my immediate thought was, "Yes!" but upon almost instantaneous reflection, maybe not.

I believe this/my/all condition/s came as a sign, a marker, a big, giant neon banner saying that something in my life needed to change. If the condition were gone forever, for certain, then, although I can't imagine doing this, I might feel the longing to go back to the old life, to the way it was, to the known. The future is unknown, it's scary. It's dark in there.

But it's also the only place where "new" can be created. New and change and different. When you're happy and confident, those ideas sound like adventures, fresh and appealing. But when you're in survival, they just sound like obstacles.

Chicken or the egg?

I hate to admit it, but I've been waiting for my physical symptoms to subside before I allowed myself to celebrate. I know that's the slow way or maybe not even a way that's going to work, but it's the logical and rational way. But that's starting to change in me.

Somehow the physical symptoms are hanging on. I've changed so much in my life for the better in recent months, but my body is hanging around to make sure I'm the real deal, that this isn't just a quick fix or a change to appease my short-term self, fix my physical symptoms and go back to the way it was. I believe my physical symptoms want to see lasting change, meaningful, heartfelt, pure change (or at least the acceptance of it) before it does more work in reducing my physical symptoms.

Maybe it's this understanding that let me release this weekend. Maybe my buckets of tears allowed that floodgate to open and let go of the trying and the waiting and the expecting. It's letting go of the sadness that was the self who I no longer am. Maybe the sadness comes from not the death of the condition, but the death of my past self.

Maybe I don't need to actually kill that past self either. Maybe just let it dangle at the end of the pack. Maybe there's a follow group of stragglers who are back there, but so far back you can't see them. If you get a flat tire, even if you're in the leader group, they'll catch up with you. Don't worry or stress about that, though. You're in shape, you have a team alongside you and all around you. You'll be back up and rolling in a flash. You'll again pass the condition and your old self, but this time with ease, no hard feelings, even a wave, and a smile. A genuine smile.

Remember, without them, there would be no contrast, there would be no front or back, you'd just be out there alone—they helped get you this far. Acknowledge them, thank them. Let them ride slowly back there, keeping you peddling and going forward. Remember, it's no longer difficult, you're just cruising. You're slipstreaming off of the power of your team.

At some point, you might look back and see part of your condition has completely disappeared. Or maybe your old self was so far behind he took a wrong turn and is gone forever. That's OK. They served you well. They got you this far. Now we're upfront, we're leading the pack, but it's not a race, it's an open road and up ahead? The unknown.

Ready? I am.
    Bradley Charbonneau, 2015

Who Am I Now?

The title of this book popped out of the universe and onto a page during a conversation with Bradley after Carefree. He'd been having difficulty explaining what had happened to him at the workshop, often receiving those blank looks from people who see a changed you and can't believe you're real. I was guiding him to slow down his excitement and look for a crack of least resistance to offer a few words that might make their way in. Within a few minutes, I said, "It starts with open. Well, everything new actually starts with open."

When things like that happen, there is a brief moment of the StillSpace I spoke about in the Prologue. A feeling of gravity that makes me pay attention. Ten minutes later, I'd bought the domain name. A book title had been born!

Bradley has traveled extensively, once leaving a plum job in Europe to wander the world with the woman who is now his wife. One of the first things he taught me was the value of taking the train instead of a plane. He would take trains and buses from San Francisco, where he was living, to Los Angeles, where his parents lived. This honestly perplexed me. Who would take the slow route when you could get there faster? I'd been a get it done, get there now person who was mostly going around in circles. His influence got me to slow down, take a more meandering path, and let the surprises magically appear.

Bradley did indeed cry buckets during Carefree, and many of those tears ended up on my shirt, my sleeve, my tortilla chips...whatever was handy. I've seen it at workshops many times now. When someone finally opens their heart, it releases a fountain of tears. Tears of release, tears of anger, tears of sorrow that eventually become tears of gratitude, tears of joy, and tears of love.

* * *

I asked Bradley to answer the question of Who Am I Now? He's a writer, so he sent me a couple of deftly crafted stories. I get that it's challenging to describe yourself to others, so I used my author's privilege to add to this section. We do talk regularly about our mutual projects, and he did smear tears all over me in Carefree, thus making me imminently qualified to out him.

JOYOUS BEYOND CONDITION

Aren't you glad I didn't make the toast at your wedding?

When I first met Bradley, I recognized him from the question he'd asked during the Dr. Joe teleclass. He had an illness doctors couldn't diagnose and a treatment plan to be on prescription drugs for the rest of his life. I'm grateful he said, "no thanks!" Otherwise, he'd never have shown up as the fifth person in a condo in Carefree with four women he'd never met. His is a magical story that will help many people, and I plan to pull it out of him in an interview on his Repossible podcast[17] before the memory fades.

I'm thrilled to report that Bradley is now a happy, healthy ex-pat. If you want to know how he morphed from a depressed, overweight, seriously ill, hate-my-job guy who said yes to a 30 day write everyday experiment, into someone so happy he annoys people, check out his best-selling book, *Every Single Day*. Bradley packed up his family a year after Carefree and headed to Europe. He now lives, works, and plays in Holland and continues to travel the world.

A few weeks after Carefree, his father died, and the two of them haven't stopped talking since. His Dad, is a light-hearted guide offering practical wisdom. I love when I get a story from his son with details that include a meditation with his Dad, and I also love it when his father pops into one of my meditations!

Bradley still refuses to talk about his condition, but it is gone. He healed through meditation, and a choice to walk away from the old, to embrace a new life. There were also a few mystical interventions that yours truly assisted with!

Like so many of us, Bradley hides some of his superpowers from the world. Let's just say he sees waaaay more than he lets on, astounding people with his accurate insights.

* * *

Who Am I Now? By Bradley Charbonneau 2019

My first thought after reading that forum post I wrote after Carefree? "Oh, that poor guy!" How he was suffering! If only he'd known how close he was to crossing over to the other side, he might have relaxed a little, might have let go, might have let it happen.

I have struggled to write this "Who Am I Now?" section because I can't always believe that the guy mentioned elsewhere in this book, also called Bradley Charbonneau, is the same guy who's writing this now.

Who I Am Now has both nothing and everything to do with the Old Bradley.

Everything, because Old Bradley got me to where I am today.

Nothing, because I feel like I have little in common with that guy.

When it was happening, I never thought I would say this. "Today, I'm thankful for my physical condition and my dad's passing. Without them, I wouldn't have escaped my mundane life, risen up, taken the leap of faith."

Before I go blabbing on about how enjoyable and easy and stressless my current life is, can we revisit that guy from just a few years ago? I don't want to do it, but I think it'll be good for you. OK, fine, it'll be good for me, too.

He was hoping. He was dreaming. He was wishing, doing lots of trying and pushing and expecting. He was also sometimes scared and frustrated and angry.

Four years after Carefree, I can say these things: I am magical. I am powerful. I see, I hear, I feel. I write, create, discover, laugh, cry, dance, and tiptoe through a dandelion patch of dreams.

I can do anything. I can do everything. I can choose to do this over that. I'm in control, yet happily floating down a stream of love.

Am I getting too sappy for you? Just wait.

I see sparkles that drift down from the trees. I see into people's hearts and know who they are. I hear music in the wind.

It's not just happy. Happy is when your burrito is ready, and you got extra tortilla chips.

This is a more profound, thunderstruck, momentous, and overwhelming joy that I wasn't sure existed outside of 2-year-olds and dogs.

Who Am I Now?

I'm me.

I am that guy from the past—I thank him for sending me here.

I am that guy from the present. This magical, deliriously delicious delicacy of the present day.

How did I get here?

It starts with something both simple and hard to understand. One of those things where I look back and ask, "Seriously? Was that all?"

It starts with a mindset shift. A perspective modification. A sliver of a chance my future self might be right there inside me.

It starts with open.

13

The Absence of Fear is Peace-Monday, May 4, 2015

Did you know if you are really still, you can hear butterfly wings?

My daughter, Meaghan, could always walk up to any animal and be entirely at ease. Whether it's horses, dogs, snakes, elephants, or giraffes, you name it; she's cool with them. When she was around four years old, I bought two books to help to explain what it means when animals and birds and insects show up in your life. Both *Animal Speak* by Ted Andrews[18] and *Medicine Cards* by Jamie Sams & David Carson[19] are dog eared books that have moved with us five times. As a child, Meaghan instinctively knew the meaning of animals, and has a deep affinity with wolves.

At the age of eighteen, she manifested a private wolf encounter in northern Quebec. The weather was slightly misty, so the rest of the tour didn't show up, making the experience entirely her own. All the animals at the facility had been injured or rescued and could now live safely in their natural habitat. A guide walked her through the process, answering her many questions. She was calm, sure, and in her element while playing with this young grey wolf. I watched in wonder, loving her beaming smile. When it was over, she had this aura of awe and a desire to never wash her hands, despite the wet hairy mess on her fingers! I witnessed the transformation of her being, and it took all of 45 minutes.

* * *

I didn't have that ease with animals or nature until Carefree. I started having nightmares about snakes when I was very, very little. Growing up in rural New Brunswick, Canada, the chances of me seeing a snake and not having my mother know about it was highly unlikely. We didn't get a TV until I was four years old, and it only had two channels, so my seeing a snake in the cartoons we were allowed to watch would hardly invoke the terror I experienced in my dreams.

I do clearly recall the first time I saw a snake coiled up in the sunshine near the gravel pit that was close to our house. I was probably eight, not two! I was with my sisters and refused to turn my back to it, afraid if I moved, it would strike out or follow me. I don't know how I made it home, and one of the sadnesses of having two deceased sisters is the fact that I cannot ask them what they recall.

Snake nightmares followed me all my life, although they diminished as I got older. Replaced by dreams of levitating, and others that we sisters always attempted to analyze at the dinner table. Our boyfriends were often weirded out by our ability to recall dreams, and our willingness to talk about them.

My mother recalls that my night terrors often included the snakes slithering over and inside my body. I have a clear memory from around age six of waking up and feeling a large snake slide up the left side of my body and being frozen with fear. Oddly though, I'd never been bitten in a dream.

My snake experiences started coming to light during the *Lost Decade*. I'd be on my chiropractor's table; he'd give me an adjustment, and snakes would leave my body. Lots and lots of them! Some of the personal work I've done includes a past-life as a Shaman in Central Mexico. It was fascinating to see a bird/snake creature in a hypnotic state only to discover Quetzalcoatl, the feathered serpent, and one of the most important gods of Mesoamerica.

* * *

I often describe my meditations and mystical experiences to Meaghan. She researches those, pinpointing locations, photos, and historical facts that help me understand where I've been and what I've seen. My friend Joe calls me a Dharma Feeler, someone who experiences first and gains the understanding later.

Meaghan can take complex topics and distill them into one or two simple lines. She listens, comprehends, and makes connections better than any computer. How? Because she has an element, the internet doesn't, an incredible connection to the vast complexity of the universe, which she doesn't consider complex. She is quietly brilliant and my favorite sounding board.

* * *

Even though Bradley had flown out early on Monday, Leanne, Jeannie, and I had a fabulous lunch with his sister. She gave us the free tickets to the Phoenix Botanical Gardens, the perfect spot for our Magical Monday. It rained on our way there, yet stopped while we explored. Rain in the desert always wakes up the wildlife...

May 5, 2015-email

THE ABSENCE OF FEAR IS PEACE-MONDAY, MAY 4, 2015

Hi, Dr. Joe (and the rest of you wonderful people),

I gather the standard opening line is "you're not going to believe this but." However, I know you will believe it, and even better, it doesn't matter to me whether you do or not.

First, get used to hearing from me because I had the most miraculous, poignant, loving, fun, delightful, outstanding, transformational time in Carefree.

I realize as I write this on the plane home on Tuesday that I came in with a very big, very powerful desire to become supernatural. I wasn't there to manifest a car, although I truly understand that a car is miraculous for many people. I leave behind judgment, I leave with acceptance.

So, Dr. Joe, you told me to choose a superpower, and I did. The fact that I was too scared to finish my Mind Movie until Wednesday night is no longer relevant. I did it. I went larger than life, and that is what I got.

Multiplied by 10,000.

Going that big made all the small things along the way unbelievably easy.

I have 1000 stories, and it's only been a week. Stories about dying and rebirth and understanding what it's like to be completely and totally loved. Stories of becoming a fairy and a dragon and entering a realm I never knew I was part of. Miraculous, to say the least.

So back to the snake. My friends, Jeanie and Leanne, and I decided to go to the Phoenix Botanical Gardens on Monday as we'd built in an extra day for fun after the event. Yes, we manifested free tickets!

My senses were so heightened, and I felt so attuned to nature that the day was endlessly surreal. The power of rows of saguaro cacti on the mountain pouring into me, and me bowing to their majesty. Standing in front of a bush and letting the birds and butterflies come to me. I'd learned to let things come to me, and when I am very still, they most certainly do. Tiny finches were in the bush, gold and red; rabbits were on the ground, and then in came the hummingbird. It went by my head, then shot straight up in the air a good 100-150 feet and then dive-bombed straight down again, swooped by me and then the show off did it again for the sheer joy of the whole thing!

That would've been fun enough, but my life is now like those TV ads where they go, "but wait, there's more!"

A man walked up to ask if we'd like to see a snake. Jeannie was up the path with her camera in a heartbeat. Leanne practically passed out, confessed her lifelong horror of snakes, and walked the other way.

My mother will attest to the fact that I started having dreams of snakes before I ever saw one. We didn't have a TV, so I hadn't seen anything in this lifetime to evoke such terror. I can vividly recall many scary dreams as a young girl, waking up screaming because I could feel snakes in my body, slithering all over me. I'd be frozen in my bed, unable to move, barely breathing.

Jeannie knew this, so she was quite surprised when I walked up the path with her. I stood about three feet away, quietly in complete communion with a five-foot-long Kingsnake. I watched it move, admired its grace, and even allowed it to come towards me. Then I thought "not ready for contact just yet," so he raised his head, turned, and off he slithered.

Dr. Joe, it wasn't that I was being brave and decided to conquer some lifelong fear. I just walked up and admired the snake, like it was a cute puppy. The crazy thing is when Jeannie and I talked after it was like I couldn't remember having a fear of snakes-at all.

THE ABSENCE OF FEAR IS PEACE-MONDAY, MAY 4, 2015

My fear wasn't just gone, it was like it had never existed!
How did this happen?

It was the final meditation on Sunday. The Breath. This was where I did get brave and did make a decision to overcome my fear. Two snakes had appeared in my meditation, and I allowed them to twine up each leg and then entwine at the base of my spine and then move up my spine as one snake and into my brain. At some point, I saw them for who they are, I saw them for what they have taught me, and then the snakes were caressing my face, and I'm looking at them with love and gratitude. Then they left, and the meditation continued.

I didn't remember my old story when the man said, "do you want to see a snake?"

The absence of fear is peace. I walk with grace upon the earth. With love and utmost gratitude.

Adwynna

Who Am I Now?

I didn't go to Carefree to work on a fear of snakes. Never crossed my mind. This gift, and how it unfolded, was an unexpected side-effect of the breakthrough on May 1st.

So much changes when you know you are safe.

There are deeper and deeper levels of everything. The more I allow, the more I open to more, the more I end up feeling. And feeling creates the emotion, which is energy in motion.

It isn't our thoughts that bring our creations home, it's how we feel about those thoughts.

CAREFREE, IT STARTS WITH OPEN

The feelings I *thought* I was reaching for to open my heart and remove the heaviness I carried into Carefree was NOTHING like the feeling of love I experienced when I finally merged with the love of oneness. I thought I knew what gratitude was until I finally felt it, sobbing and saying thank you, thank you, thank you for all these miracles.

* * *

Because of Carefree, I've nicknamed the day after any event *Magical Monday*. For the entire day, I just go where I'm guided, and wow, I've had some fabulous ones, three of them with Leanne.

Simply allow whatever happens to happen, and you will get a litany of cool, unusual, joyous things to add to an already overflowing bucket!

Honestly, it's the most fun you can have. Detach from your phone, get out in nature, talk to new people, and ask them what they recommend you do next. Follow the breadcrumbs and watch as they turn into sparkling fairy dust.

Sample new foods swim with your clothes on (or off) because the waterfall is right there! Ride on the Ferris wheel, say yes to joining strangers for a meal, and don't be surprised if you become lifelong friends. Laugh at billboards or signs that suddenly have a deeper meaning, order something you'd usually say no to, then celebrate when they give it to you for free.

Gift a Magical Monday to yourself at least four times a year, regardless of whether it's tied to an event, or on a Monday. I guarantee you a magical day of serendipity and sacred encounters.

And a ton of laughs!

* * *

THE ABSENCE OF FEAR IS PEACE-MONDAY, MAY 4, 2015

For more ideas on how to create your own Magical Monday, plus extra stories from our day, check out resources.adwynna.com

IV

Beyond Carefree

Many people have seen her. They've just been waiting for her to see herself.
Karen Kessler, June 2015

14

What Are You Open To?

My mission is to guide people more and more into alignment with the light of their inner being. The Everyman and Everywoman who discovers my work, and suddenly see an opening, a glimpse of more.

I love it when the lights go on behind people's eyes, then their hearts open, and they see who they can be. Those who wake up to the realization that what they once considered to be impossible is now possible.

The first thing people want to do once they feel better, heal themselves, or discover a method that worked for them is to share it with someone. They feel so great and so free they are bursting with excitement and enthusiasm.

When I got home from Carefree, I was that person. The world seemed so bright and beautiful, my heart was open with love, and my body vibrating with joy. I was flying high, and it all seemed so simple and easy.

I forgot that nothing much had changed in my house. I'd only been gone a week, and when I left, I was depressed and resentful. Imagine being a member of my family and trying to adjust to the new me? They'd said goodbye to a quiet and sad person on a Tuesday and were met by a blissfully happy person eight days later.

My transformation was so complete that even my dog didn't recognize me! Baxter, who adores me and typically goes nuts when I've been away, casually sniffed my leg and walked away. It took him a day or two to adjust to the energy of new me, and our bond became even stronger.

The people around me took longer to adjust and embrace the new me, and some never have.

* * *

People who have similar stories to mine discovered the same thing; our pets quickly love our new selves while our people often don't. Although it's a head-scratcher to think people will say no thank you to health, happiness, and calm, it happens quite often.

Sometimes, it's the over-exuberance of the delivery, and sometimes our new self threatens to shake them out of complacency.

To be fair, my friends and family had watched me go to events before and come back all hyped up, only to see me revert back to my former self rather quickly. There is a lot of doubt around how long the good feelings from peak experiences will last and how those will play out in "real life."

* * *

One of my most significant AHA's was learning the science behind why those good feelings can disappear. Known as Hebb's Rule, the phrase "neurons that fire together, wire together" is often said by Dr. Joe and is attributed to Neuropsychologist Donald Hebb, who first used it in

1949 to describe how pathways in the brain are formed and reinforced through repetition.

Every time we learn something, new neural networks are created in our brains. Profound experiences, like the ones I'd had in Carefree, create stronger networks as neurons begin to fire and wire differently. Those neural networks *need to be reinforced,* or our brains will revert to the path of least resistance, meaning we will go back to being the way we were. Within three days!

This knowledge answered a question I had pondered for a long time. It explained why I hadn't been able to sustain my excitement and commitment to change from previous retreats, courses, or books I'd read. I now knew I needed to maintain the practice of my new habits to have the old neurons in my brain prune away so the new neurons could become the new pathway.

* * *

It often helps us understand how we change and get better at something by using sport as the analogy. Even if you haven't played a sport for a while, you can easily insert something else into this story. Perhaps you go to the gym or have started a yoga practice. Maybe you used to burn grilled cheese sandwiches, and now you can flambé saganaki complete with a hearty *Oompah!* We've all started something new and chosen to put in the time and intention to get better at it.

My sport of choice is tennis. I started as an adult and played for fifteen years with an inconsistent forehand stroke. It was a dreadful-looking thing, yet it was competent enough for me to have progressed in my game from a late-blooming beginner to a person who could competently play at the A level in tennis leagues.

Like other aspects of my life, my will was strong enough to get me through, even though my foundation was weak.

Unfortunately, my forehand would crack under pressure, and my sloppy technique would creep into the game, causing wild misses and match losses. Not to mention frustration and a few glares from my poor doubles partners.

One day, a former top tennis professional took me on a court and dropped tennis balls in front of me for two hours. Not once did he feed a ball off of his racquet, and he only allowed me to use my forehand. Over and over and over, I hit balls with my new grip, stroke, and stance. I wasn't permitted to look where my balls landed; I was to focus on moving my feet to put myself in the right position to be able to hit the ball at the same "sweet" spot on my racquet every single time. Then I had to follow that swing through and TRUST that the ball would land where I was aiming.

Those two hours changed my game.

It took a few months to be able to use this new forehand effectively. Along the way, I struggled because my performance in match results declined. I kept with it, though, and this was long before I'd heard of Dr. Joe.

What do I have now? An ingrained physical embodiment of how to hit a solid forehand. The neural pathway is established. When my game goes awry, I can go back to the basics of what I've been taught and deliberately slow down my swing to keep the ball in play. I have a foundation on which to build.

So, what's next?

Some people are content to play a solid game or believe this is as far as their talent will take them.

Me? I always want to go to the next level. In tennis and in life. Which means standing on my foundation and adding more power, variety, and depth.

Who Am I Now?

Knowledge is power, but only if we apply it.

Coming back from Arizona as Miss Bliss, I knew if I wanted those fantastic feelings to continue, I needed to reinforce what it took to create them in the first place. I knew I needed to meditate every single day. This became my commitment to all of my future selves...I would find the time to meditate regardless of what was happening in my day.

The very first question people ask me about daily meditations is, "how much time does it take?" I no longer know the answer. I just do it. For someone starting out, any length of time is better than not doing it at all. Start with what works for you now and add in what works for you later. I typically plan for a one-hour meditation, but I've had days when I've been busy and get 10 minutes in. The key is commitment and consistency, trusting that every small change you make adds up to significant results over time.

It also helps to reinforce a new habit when we take time to celebrate the milestones along the way.

* * *

I was impressed with Bradley's write everyday habit during Carefree. It could be 11:30 pm, and he would take out his tablet and bang out a blog post for the day before the clock struck midnight. He carried a little notebook and would jot down potential topics that popped in during the day, taking inspiration from conversations, or funny signs we'd see that he'd photograph to accompany his blog. Everything was grist for his writing mill.

What I loved most is he wasn't attached to what he wrote, how good it was, whether he'd edited it, or if anyone would even read it. For Bradley, the habit of daily writing morphed into a whole new life and career. It isn't the habit; it's all the crazy cool, super amazing things that are happening for him along the way!

It took a few months for people to be convinced the new me was here to stay. I began to integrate what had happened and embody my experiences in my daily life. Instead of overwhelming people with wild tales of my meditations, or the everyday miracles I saw around me, I started to wait for the crack of least resistance to appear.

15

Dancing on Both Ends of the Stick

Yesterday was pink, today is yellow. I wonder what color tomorrow will be?

A spiritual awakening has many ups and downs. The difference is a new ability to see the downs as information leading to more. I moved more quickly out of dark places, yet the dark areas were still there, yearning to show me their role in my creations.

When my sister Tracey died in 1994, I was plunged into grief so deep and overpowering I thought I'd never re-surface. Connor was ten months old, and my love for him kept me grounded. I see now that he held the tether that kept me here on this earth.

In the midst of it all, I started catching glimpses of the fine line between my physical reality and non-physical reality. It seemed as though the only thing that separated me from my pain and loss here and the peace on the other side was this door I could easily walk through. I could feel myself wanting to slip over, yet I resisted the temptation.

How I wish I'd surrendered to that place and walked through that door. The amount of suffering and sadness I could have saved myself if I'd only known...

It's not a one-way door.

Carefree blew the doors wide open. My final two nights in Arizona were the first of many where I wave around the universe. I call it "wave" as a way to describe being in an extended, altered state that is not part of any formal meditation. I'm relaxed and open, and willing to go where I'm taken. Not asleep, nor fully awake.

I often travel inter-dimensionally, encountering Light Beings, and mythical creatures. Mostly, I experience higher levels of awareness of reality. Waves of energy rock my body, resulting in unusual physical responses. Often my body will sit straight up and immediately fall back down on the pillow, sometimes three or four times in a row. Our rational fear of falling backward would kick in if I were to try and demonstrate that in a waking state. Not to mention, I don't have the abs for it!

On those first two "wave" nights, certain people would pop into my awareness. I'd ask them what they needed and give it to them, whether it was healing, or answers to questions. Sometimes people said no, even though we were communicating on a spiritual plane. Once I checked in on someone, only to be immediately blanketed in my bed by a protective dragon. It was clear I wasn't to go anywhere near that person!

Although I wasn't sleeping the way people would typify a good night's rest, I still had enormous energy in my days. I thrived on a few hours of sleep and loved the ease at which I could walk between worlds.

***

Then I started having mystical experiences in my awake state.

Today I walked through a vortex of my former selves while taking Baxter for a stroll.

A night of sadness. Up 2:45-4:30am. BEC med, powerful. I am the egg. I have manifested my object. I am my object.

It's funny-the pen doesn't flow at all. It's stiff and awkward. Sadness is a sticky substance.

It is also the loneliest of the emotions. Oh sure, anxiety and depression get all the attention-heck they get official medical diagnoses, prescription drugs, and government action plans.

Sadness, well sadness gets nothing because it doesn't get noticed. We carry it around like a giant sucking weight on our heart and attempt to put one foot in front of the other.

You cannot outrun sadness because it is softly enveloping you like a dewy mist. After a while, you don't even bother to shake the moisture off yourself. You just walk around smelling like an old wet dog.

The new me, a woman who is now 12 days old, decided to walk her dog in a different direction. More open fields which made him run and laugh and be happy. Even he gets bored with the same path every day. New sights, new sounds are very energizing.

I crossed the road to take the path by the church. At the crossroad, I turned right to walk what would typically be backward towards home.

I could feel the familiar pull of entering another space and time, yet this time I was not in a meditation. I walked through a heavier fog, although it was a blindingly clear morning. Picked a flower, waited for a couple to pass. They smiled. They all smile at me now.

As I walked, I passed by myself. All the hundreds of me's who had walked that path in sadness. Each had a discernible energetic blueprint, some dressed in winter clothes, some with head down, walking, but not seeing.

I felt them as we walked by each other, them not noticing me except for maybe a glimmer of who they were to become.

Because it must have started there. They must have created an opening, a tiny crack of intention, a glimpse into their future self (selves).

It is them I have to thank. With every sad footstep, they created the path for me.

The next time I pass them, I will do so without pity or sorrow. I will pass them with gratitude for the foundation they laid for me to shine.

Who Am I Now?

June 2015-Journal Entry

Waking Up

Yellow is the color of joy. Today I am surrounded by that after an epic meditation. I am officially out of superlatives.

I fell asleep after the mediation, and woke up with a huge rush of energy, leaving my crown, gushing out of my body and leaving my head. Almost jolted out of bed!

I was enveloped in yellow, flowers are everywhere, and I just started to laugh.

Here I am, lying in bed on a Monday morning at 7:17 AM, laughing my ass off. Hilarious way to start today.

Then I flitted around the universe, sending healing, love, and light and whatever gifts people are able to receive. I send it to all the people that come to mind.

I get up and have orange juice, pull the cut-up pineapple out of the refrigerator. Think to myself, "I'm hungry." I make myself scrambled eggs.

I'm laughing because everything I've chosen is yellow.

It's difficult to convey how incredibly natural it feels to live this way.

To have perpetual awareness of how much more is around us all the time, how much bigger we are. There is so much we have access to that can allow us to live fully. To have joyful, healthy, fascinating, and impactful lives.

It turns out there is a lot to be debunked about our interpretations of the spiritual world, and perhaps my work on this planet is to help with that?

How do we start? What do we do?

Open those doors and enter unafraid. Know we are safe.

What I know for sure is how beautifully I'm taken care of at all times, even amid struggle and pain. While *waving* one night beside a beach in Mexico, I was taken back through my life and saw how everything I'd experienced was gorgeously orchestrated to allow me to be exactly where I am. I deeply understood the death of my sisters, the struggles I'd had around self-worth and acceptance of my purpose on this earth, and in this particular body. It reminded me of the life-review people describe in a Near Death Experience (NDE).

* * *

When people I'd check in on during meditations would say no to offers of healing or help, I used to believe that how open we are here is actually reflected there. There is truth to that, and yet, from the higher perspective I gained in Mexico, I believe they may have declined my offer because they had chosen to have the experience they were having and had yet to fully reap its rewards.

After all, how could I appreciate all that's been happening for me now if I hadn't experienced the opposite?

I was sharing a story with a group, and someone asked me, "how do I get to have experiences like you've had?" Another shared that she could manifest easily in certain aspects of her life, such as her health and her job, yet she really struggled to find a life partner. In attempting to answer her own question, she offered up, "I know, I know. Let go, surrender, have no expectations."

I could feel the frustration at not having what they most wanted. I heard words that were still mostly concepts, not embodied emotional processes.

It was more of a social gathering than a teaching opportunity, so I allowed this question to sit for a while. I waited for the crack of an opening to appear and an answer to land. The one they would hear and take in and act on.

> *"How do I get to have experiences like you've had? How do I manifest more easily?"*

My answer:

> *"Treat it like a playground."*

16

Rear-Ended Blessing

Five days after I got home from Carefree, my car was rear-ended on a bright sunny, Mother's Day. I strained my wrist and jammed my shoulder because my right hand was on the gear shift. Doctors diagnosed me with whiplash and a mild concussion. All I could do for weeks was write without editing because I couldn't read, watch TV, or be on any screens.

Email to Dr. Joe-May 17, 2015

You're not going to believe this (ha), but I left Carefree on a phenomenal high and got rear-ended on Mother's Day. It turned out to be an astounding gift. Although going forward, I would prefer less jolting presents.

The accident itself is not particularly relevant. I was in a good place, having only recently danced my way out of the local grocery store about to enjoy an evening with my children and some friends my son had adopted for the day who didn't have mothers around.

There is no trauma to clear around the accident, no trapped negative emotions. Adrenalin performed its role. I remained calm, assessed the situation, and took the trembling 17-year-old boy to a nearby parking lot to exchange information.

It didn't look like a whole lot of damage to the car, and he said once or twice, "I thought I hit you harder than that."

Turns out he was right.

On Monday morning, I knew I wasn't in good shape. The odd thing was, I was in great shape. My middle of the night meditation was awesome, and I wasn't feeling any real pain. However, I got woozy while out walking my dog and had some stiffness in my neck and right hand and shoulder. My mother was not impressed when I suggested I drive myself to the emergency room at the hospital, so my husband came home from work.

It was actually funny. I was so aligned I aced the baseline tests and was only diagnosed with a mild concussion and whiplash. I then went to my osteopath, who told me I my concussion was far from "mild" and released some of the physical trauma.

I was told to rest my mind, not watch any TV, computer screens or read. I was to relax and let my mind be still.

And therein lies the gift.

I hadn't been able to figure out where I would ever find the time to capture the hundreds of things that happened to me while I was in Carefree. This concussion allowed me to turn off my regular internal editor and just write without reading any of it!

I got to meditate. The meditations were even more epic than Carefree. I got to walk in nature and continue my newfound communion with it, and it's creatures. I chucked out everything ugly in my closet and drawers.

I made space in my life.

The past few weeks have been as transcendent and brilliant as the five days I spent at your event.

You see, Dr. Joe, my mental acuity was my pride. I have a thick layer of analytical mind. My entire life, I have read everything that presented itself to me. I am an information junkie. I love facts and details and enjoy making connections between all of the various things I have learned along the way.

The part of my brain that seemed to be the most injured was the part where I access facts and details.

I had trouble recalling my postal code to make my insurance claim. Even now, I can feel myself going to a specific section in my left brain when someone asks me a question, and it requires going to get a fact or piece of information. It's hazy there and sometimes blank. I can get there, but I feel my brain searching for it as opposed to it being a quick recall.

This hasn't particularly concerned me. In fact, I found it rather amusing.

I sleep for a few hours and get up and meditate in the middle of the night. Sometimes I stay up and write. Sometimes I go back to bed.

One night I was meditating without the sound of your voice. I asked myself if I could learn to speak with my heart. I spent the meditation doing that, arguing briefly with my mind. I could feel my entire world-changing. It was very blessed and very profound.

I have been speaking with my heart ever since, and when I don't, I feel it immediately.

I've worked with people in energy psychology or whatever they're calling it these days for about 19 years. My intuition has always been strong, and my sessions have been very guided. I have a tendency to look to external explanations for what is happening to me or my clients. Sometimes during the session and almost always after.

Now I'm doing sessions for people and relying entirely on my own internal knowledge, fully trusting my guidance to bring in what is perfect for each and every client.

Sessions are taking on a whole new level!

I'm trying to find words to convey this:

By losing my mind to a concussion, I could've been grumpy, could have moaned about all my lost time and all the things that I was going to do. But I didn't.

I used this time to continue in the state of grace I'd brought back from Carefree.

I learned to answer questions, do sessions without access to any external piece of information.

Everything had to come from within.

After a couple of days of doing this, I looked at my daughter and told her what was going on for me. I looked at her and said, 'I know a lot.' She nodded; she already knew that. I was the one never thinking I knew enough.

All those years of data accumulation have assimilated into my being. I can access that and much, much more easily and effortlessly.

I know enough. I am enough.

I've never said those words before in my life beyond a few feeble attempts at affirmations that never had a home for them to land.

Thank you for providing me with the platform to find my way home.

Who Am I Now?

I still have to remind myself to speak, lead, and guide from my heart. I'm a human being, after all, and I get curve balls tossed my way. When you've just been hit with a hardball, natural conditioning is going to kick in. We're going to lose our tempers, over-react, say things we later wish we hadn't. When we're stressed, our thinking brain, where thoughts naturally gather, will pull us in many directions.

I have practiced the art of being in alignment, and I don't like how it feels when I'm not. When things go wrong, it may take a few minutes, a few hours or a nudge from a friend to remind me that I'm not showing up as my best self.

When I finally notice I'm out of alignment, I take a few minutes and consciously move my energy into my heart center, creating heart-brain coherence. When I do this, my body calms down, dire situations seem less complicated, conversations flow, and the words I use are readily received by the listener.

* * *

Although I've always been comfortable doing presentations or public speaking, I'd seen certain people on stage who could engage audiences and maintain their energy in ways I wanted to emulate. I wanted to do more teaching and speaking, plus I needed to be way more at ease on video.

I chose to take a program called Stage and Story from ChooseRE-SULTS Inc. that kicked out habits gained from corporate presentation training and debunked the "you need to memorize your speech," I'd associated with public speaking. The aim was to create authentic, compelling speakers who were completely at ease in front of any sized audience.

For the first time ever, I made the decision to sign up for a program in about five minutes. It wasn't a small thing either. The course took six months and required travel and financial commitment. How was I able to decide so quickly?

I, as my present-self, checked in with my future-self and asked her, *"Did I take this program to become you?* My future-self said yes, so I signed up!

Wow! How much time can I save with this new rapid decision making technique? A lot, as it's turned out. Who knew that creating my future-self, and practicing becoming her in meditation, would lead to a way for my present-self to make easier choices?

* * *

One of the first things I learned in Stage & Story was a skill called Trainer State to connect with my audience and trust my unconscious mind to guide me. When I'm in Trainer State, I'm congruent with my energy, the energy of the audience and I'm speaking from my heart. It took me months to master this skill. Now I can move into that state of being within a few minutes. In the beginning, I had to remember to stop what I was accustomed to doing and consciously apply my new skill.

Even though I could see my future-self on stage teaching and speaking, I still needed to implement the skills in order to make it part of my 3D reality!

Want something to be easier? Get clear on your vision of yourself doing it, being it and enjoying it. (That vision is your future-self by the way).

Whatever decisions need to be made can be easier and more accurate when you take the time to connect with your future-selves. Let them be your guide.

To receive a free gift from ChooseRESULTS Inc. created specifically for Carefree readers, go to resources.adwynna.com Chapter 16.

17

Parallel Lives

Leanne is a lasting gift from Carefree. Like Bradley, she'd responded to my post for roommates and had driven from Wyoming. Which is not exactly close by! She unnerved me for the entire workshop with her ability to materialize from the ether. She'd be across the room and then suddenly be behind or in front of me. Quietly observant, wickedly funny, and supremely astute, Leanne tells it like it is. She's been to hell and left it all there. She also sleeps like a hibernating bear.

Leanne sent this email to the condo roommates on May 10, 2015. It certainly explained her ability to appear out of nowhere, not to mention that bear!

> *Remember the parallel lives theory? This is something that I did not tell you. It has to do with this whole Native American thing we have going on.*
>
> *In this context, on one side of me, I had my past. (Adwynna), who spoke of being uncomfortable, even fearful of this. When I was in my late 20's, I spent a lot of time on the Pine Ridge Indian Reservation doing sweats with a Medicine Man. This was*

my formal introduction to their beliefs and how they worked in the world. I was an archaeologist at the time and spent hours with ancient artifacts. I dealt with elders from the Arapahoe and Shoshone Tribes being a white intermediary into their culture and dealing with these ancient remains.

In short, I was immersed in Native American energy, culture, spirituality, and time. What I saw and experienced was enormously profound and powerful. It was at this time that I was gifted my first healing abilities.

It is the first time I had a true out of body experience where I traveled. I talked to animals, to Gods, to the wind, and to the directions.

One night in a very weird movie theater in Vermont, I saw the movie PowWow Highway, and this movie and the music in it, became my touchstone to what I knew, and even who I was.

The medicine man really didn't want me around, because he was letting me in on so many "secretes," but he was told that he could not turn me away. I was a stranger in a strange land. Out of place, and not fully equipped or prepared for what was happening. Quite frankly, it scared the ever-loving shit out of me. I was young. I knew so deeply that this was "the real thing," and because it scared me, I tucked it away in a safe place. I stopped going to sweats, and would not join in conversations about them. I refuse to smudge my rooms with sweet sage. My tobacco ties are buried in a drawer somewhere. I won't pick up eagle feathers. I took my quilts from the sundance and put them in a box in the basement. I have actively, and with great respect, turned my back on all of this for the past 25 years.

Then I went to Carefree.

The Native American thing was so far removed from my life that I never gave it a second thought that I would be surrounded by *this power. On my drive to the workshop, when the people selling jewelry on the bridge crossing the Colorado River, said, "Welcome back," I thought it was "cute." While in Sedona, I was flat out told by a Native American, "it is time for you to come back to us." We had two drumming ceremonies. They danced and called in eagles, and great spirits. I saw hawks and pigs, and yes, even snakes. In one of the meditations, a snake came into my brain and ate my fear.*

Not the fear of snakes, my fear of this spirit.

Back to the context, on the other side of me, I saw my possible future (Jeannie) of how embracing this once again was possible. I felt her ease with it, and observed how she embraced it, and it has significant meaning for her. If it was safe for Jeannie, maybe it could be safe for me too. So while I was in Carefree, I was looking at examples of both possibilities, of two realities, of my past, of my future, hiding or embracing, I felt smack damn in the middle of IT, and it being ONLY the present moment, but it was evolving and revolving, and spinning....as we were speaking and experiencing.

This was getting interesting to me. The edges were blurring. The past, the future, and the present were so tangible, in NO time, I could touch them.

On my way home from Carefree, I spent two full days on a reservation. I went to Canyon de Chelly, and interacted with history, with antiquity, and with the people who live there today. I went here to find some grounding to bring me back. I biked and hiked. I sat on the ground with my back against a rock, under a tree, and meditated. Here I knew that I was with everyone who had ever walked there, all in one present moment, and received a blessing and a welcoming home. I drove for miles and miles

through this land, down long and peaceful highways, seeing so much beauty everywhere I looked.
  And put myself back together.
  I got home, and many parts of it sucked, truth be told. But it is all good, nevertheless.

More of the me who is me, perhaps the me who I turned my back on, is becoming ever more present.

Yesterday was my birthday, and my family at home was kind of scattered. Today being Mothers Day, they had me open some presents. I got a nice sweater and even an Apple Watch. But my eldest daughter gave me something hard to find, not available on Amazon, has monetary value because it is a collector's item, but most importantly, filled with thought (———————, as in energy, not matter)...a DVD of the movie PowWow Highway.

Expect the unexpected.

Who Am I Now?

I am constantly amazed at how many of us are hiding ourselves and what it is we are hiding from. We had two Native American ceremonies during the workshop and Leanne didn't say a word; even though Jeannie and I were sharing our feelings openly.

  Over time I learned that Leanne was married to a controlling man and really wanted out. It all seemed so complicated, yet she persisted in doing her own inner work. She invested in herself, creating the person she wanted to become in 5D, even though there was a large gap between that and her current 3D reality.

  At the end of the workshop in Carefree we spent a magical evening watching an electrical storm and getting to know each other. Since then we've developed a deep friendship. We've helped each other emerge into our true selves, supported each other's growth, and had some fun along the way.

***

I insisted on taking before and after photos of everyone at Carefree, so we have a record of the weight of sadness that Leanne walked in with. I also have a photo of her two years later, glowing with love and vibrancy, at peace with her choices, excited for what is coming.

This is transformation, and it's never a straight line.

When we are in our stuckness, getting out and living a new life feels daunting. Like it will take forever. Yet, in no time, Leanne is free of her marriage, living in a home she loves, using her gifts as a Transformational Healer & Medical Intuitive.

Most of us beat ourselves up for what hasn't happened yet, so it's good to stop once in a while and acknowledge how far we've come. To say thank you to all of our former selves for their courage and tenacity.

In case Leanne hasn't celebrated herself recently, let's do that with her.

***

To see Leanne's (and Bradley's and Adwynna's) before and after photos check out the Chapter bonuses at resources.adwynna.com Pay close attention to our eyes!

18

Alone on the Planet

"I see myself the same way, always, since I was a very young girl. On stage, alone. I always seem shimmery, like I am a light. I have never known what I'm saying."
  Journal Entry December 29, 2014

My earliest memories of "who do you want to be when you grow up?" consist of me on a stage alone with a massive audience, and no one is saying a word. Yet I've always known the audience is deeply moved and connected.

This dream of mine is interwoven into so much of my writing and conversations that to read any of it may sound like I've lived my life with perpetual stage fright.

Exactly the opposite!

I love to teach, speak, and inspire. I am connected and alive on stage. I live for the moment when the lights go on for the audience…and by lights, I mean the light in their heart, shining out of their eyes.

* * *

Much of my adult life has consisted of me trying to find my voice, figure out my unique message. What is it I'm supposed to be teaching or speaking about? Believe me, I have lifetimes of stories, tips, advice, and interstellar guidance. Enough to help people with the steps and processes that change lives.

I do magical one-on-one sessions with clients, and I've taught and coached people to become their authentic selves. Many of those same people have cajoled, encouraged, and supported me while watching me do great work behind the scenes.

It's incredibly rewarding to watch people blossom, yet the vision of myself on that stage kept calling.

The only thing was…I was trying to logically figure out what I was saying, and it was making me crazy!

This conundrum led to years of being frustrated and confused, living my life feeling powerless, and even cowardly. I know I procrastinated and made excuses; excellent, well-crafted, articulate ones in fact.

I have given up on this dream many times. Did regular jobs lived a normal life.

Normal is a weak, tasteless watered down drink of the true essence of you.

Every time I made a choice for others instead of myself, each time I took a job for the wrong reasons, I chiseled away at my dreams. When you let your dreams die, you start the slow, painful process of dying yourself.

***

Within the stories of mystical experiences and everyday miracles are moments of struggle, pain, worry, hiding, and a LOT of procrastination.

Although I was enjoying a magical life, I still had things to sort in my life here on earth.

> *June 14, 2015-Email to Bradley*
>
> *Do you ever wake up and wonder if that feeling of being alone will ever go away? So yes, I have hit my next plateau, and yes, it's a hard slog, and my body has dug in hard with resistance. I pretty much felt like puking through my meditation last night. I overcame because I have a strong will, and I am determined not to let my old addictions win, but it was scary and lonely, and I woke up sad and angry.*
>
> *I had no one to share that with who would understand these emotions are transitory. Who would point out that I've gotten through worse and emerged chatting with a cardinal? Who would hold my hand through it and remind me of who I am?*
>
> *Maybe I need to let more people into my inner world? Everyone thinks I have my shit so together. No one knows I have days when my world collapses around me, and I feel like everything I'm doing is pointless. I am so accustomed to working my shit out on my own, and I know I can, and I know I have good people around me to help and I'm just being stupid, but today I woke up wanting more than that and it just feels like a long, lonely life ahead of me.*

That vomitous meditation proved to be groundbreaking. My body was releasing trapped energy, and it was physically painful. Many people hit walls like this, and some will stop out of fear, or bail on their meditation because it's so far from the Zen experience we believe meditation should be. I was clearing out emotions around a person who had tormented my thoughts for a few years. I'd ignored all of my intuition about staying in contact with this bully, making excuses for behavior that felt awful to the people around us and me.

Until we clear our patterns, the same people will show up in our lives, just wearing different bodysuits.

* * *

I knew from Dr. Joe that my body might fight me rather than change, as it's conditioned to keep me where I am. We learn to use our will to push through when things like this happen as it takes conscious effort to overcome old patterns.

I wasn't thinking about classroom learning in the middle of this particular meditation. I was battling an inner demon, and when my body froze into a contorted position, I recall wondering what my kids would do if they discovered their mother sitting catatonic on the couch.

In the middle of those thoughts, I started to have difficulty breathing. Not only was I frozen in one position, but I was also panicking because I couldn't get air into my lungs. Now I was wondering if my kids would find me dead on the couch!

I'd like you to appreciate the humor in this story. The reason I can tell it while laughing is that although I was in it...I was also observing it. My physical body was utterly panicking, while my higher-self awareness knew I was perfectly safe.

What did I do? I decided to ask for help. Over and over and over in my head, I said the words, *"help me, help me, help me."*

And help arrived.

Immediately.

That's what it feels like to surrender.

* * *

I am well trained, yet the tools I had in this physical realm had not been able to clear out the misery and agony of this person's abuse, lies, and betrayal. After Carefree, my patterns in relationships began to show up, and I was determined to let those go.

By asking for help – and allowing it to come – I learned to do something I'd absolutely sucked at for years. And the reward was the loving presence of guides who lifted the pain and filled my body with light.

The next time I saw my prior tormentor, she looked right through me, almost like she didn't recognize me. We ended up sitting beside each other for a surprisingly pleasant lunch. Regular contact stopped, and eventually, we faded away from each other.

This happened naturally and gradually. There was no drama, no guilt, no need for closure. We had stopped resonating at the vibration that had brought us together for years. We were simply gone from each other's life.

Who Am I Now?

Now I ask for help all the time, and it *always* arrives!

When I recount these times, I am in awe of my former self. I may not have had explanations for what was happening to me, but I trusted the process and was willing to dive deep.

Journals include many moments of clarity with answers to questions I'd had for years. After Carefree, it became clear that everything I encountered was orchestrated to guide me and give me those answers. My only job has been to remain open, trust what I receive, and allow for more.

> *May 31, 2015–Journal Entry*
> *I picked up a piece of wood on the path of my walk after the rain.*

It's a knot of a branch of a tree. I held it in my hand, examining it closely, enjoying the feel, and remembered the knot in my heart (I had walked into Carefree with.) How, by 8 years old, my dreams to sing and perform were already being chipped away. The branches I was putting out being poked at with comments, insecurities and admonitions to share the spotlight.

Don't use the glory of my voice.

Don't overpower others with my talents.

Told to blend, to shrink, to hide.

Chipping away at my branches that wanted to grow, they turned into hard knots. Conditions did not allow my tree to thrive. Like the saguaro cactus, who will not grow arms unless it has a proper foundation of nutrients, we pull inside. Our desire to branch out killed by a hostile and infertile environment. We grow, but we are the saguaro without enough resources.

A tall, lonely cactus with no arms to embrace life here.

Yet still reaching to the sky.

19

What To Do When a Tiger Walks Into Your Meditation

Whatever the Tiger wants.

May 19, 2015-Journal Entry
 I'm so quiet now. I'm invisible. Watching my gorgeous son (sun) make his coffee and his lunch for work. He moves with grace and ease. He is present with his coffee, adding cream and stirring, licking the spoon.
 Makes his sandwich with wall to wall mustard. Puts spoon in the dishwasher. Fills two bottles of water, still hasn't noticed me.
 I am so still inside my body this morning. After yesterday's frenzy of joy, this is a lovely, complete calm.
 I have no sniffles, no aches or pains. Got up (not woke up-that happened way before) around 5am. Just started to put things in order, pick up items, make the bed, arrange the pillows on my meditation couch!
 Connor is so present with his day he doesn't yet enter mine. He is not oblivious either. This isn't a tired slog. He grabbed his bag,

saw me, and smiled a moonbeam at me. He kind of waved, I waved back-I mean it's 20' to the kitchen from where I write in the dining area. He said, "How long have you been there?" Me "the whole time - I'm writing about you." He puts his hand on his heart, "I'm touched."

Smiles - says, "I've gotta run though," and off he goes into the morning.

This is a peace I could get used to, the one where he used to live.

The day before I wrote this, I had unwittingly overwhelmed Bradley in a conversation. I'd gone on and on about something he was struggling with, espousing my knowledge, not present with him at all. This probably sounds like an average day at work for many of us, with people talking over each other, sitting in meetings, competing for airspace.

Our conversation had left me feeling out of alignment...which is to say I felt yucky because I'd talked from a platform that felt true and aligned for me, yet didn't take a moment to meet him where he was. I'd talked endlessly, pushing my point into a space that wasn't prepared.

I'd sent him an apology, which confused him because he hadn't judged me the same way I'd judged myself. I later wrote:

There is power in an apology. A very real "I am sorry for going unconscious, even though I was at the higher vibration."

AHA - I just learned something! A higher vibration does not automatically make one a better or even a more evolved person...

This puzzles me, but I know it's important, so I will try and craft a question.

* * *

After that journal entry, I decided to do the Blessing of the Energy Centers (BEC) meditation, where we select symbols and place them in each energy center. The symbols are used to represent the change you are allowing yourself to embody.

I've helped many people choose and align with their symbols, as they often select one they think they should use, rather than one that has strong personal significance. For example, even though the Eye of Horus is traditionally associated with the third eye center, it may mean nothing to you, so find something that connects you to your desired outcome.

Sometimes I select the symbols for myself before a mediation, sometimes the symbols appear during the meditation, and sometimes the ones I pre-select change when I'm deep within. I trust that the symbol for me will be the one that shows up.

*＊＊

May 18, 2015-Journal Entry

Tigers adore their young, and last night, a tiger wandered into my (BEC) meditation.

This one started out hard. The end of my day was difficult. I was unfocused, upset at myself for being a "spiritual snob." A term I coined in my days with Kandis and is something that really irks me. The arrogance of those who believe they have ascended beyond us mere mortals.

Believe me, if they had ascended, they would be walking the earth with humility and grace, honoring every creature, every element in their space.

I began BEC w/ breath, and this took some work. My 2 black snakes returned, love those guys! It was messy but got a good flow.

Knew I needed to do more before the meditation began-paused. Did 2 (more rounds of the breath)– I'm on fire, panting, exhausted, ready to quit, tired of trying so hard to find my way through.

I decide to ask for help. DUH!

I ask God for help - the answer is immediate. Complete energy shift. I felt this pressure outside of myself – a Being – white light-but very solid.

Energy moved easily then, but it still took "both" of us to pull out all that judgment.

Meditation was about modesty.

Energy Center 1 was great, dragon breath to cool all that fire (thank you for that, I might have melted w/any more fire.)

Energy Center 2 was the Timepiece -something changed there from before- time escaped from the glass and just flowed.

Then Energy Center 3 solar plexus/my issue area of yesterday. I threw in intense joy and cleaned out the chakra and who wandered in but this massive tiger.

I mean the ENTIRE tiger too, not just a face or a 2D thing – an entire flippin' tiger just meanders in from my right side, flicks her tail up (deliberately) towards my heart chakra. Then she curled into a ball and went to sleep.

She certainly knows why she is there. I most certainly did not!! Tho' she is way, way cool.

Even though I'm in deep, I'm aware of my surprise and excitement.

Lying down, post-meditation, I was given a gorgeous array of orange/deep pink/yellow and one of those geo-shape things, but all soft around the edges. Lovely-powerful colors-not in my normal palette.

Received it with thanks.

Going to read about Tigers now.

CAREFREE, IT STARTS WITH OPEN

(I reviewed the material from Animal Speak)
Keynote of Tiger: Passion, power. Motherly devotion to offspring. Sensual and nocturnal.
I will manifest new adventures. I have renewed devotion and passion for life.

* * *

Turns out, the tiger came with a purpose.

A few days later, my husband was off for a bike ride. He's an avid cyclist, supports what I do, and has publicly stated that he has no interest in it. Fortunately for him, this stuff rubs off. He's been caught reporting how the *universe* supported him, or how he *manifested* something. Over time he saw how all this woo-woo stuff translated into actual things, and his crack of least resistance widened.

Back in 2015, though, the woman he'd married was suddenly very new to him. We share an aversion to conflict rooted in unstable childhoods with volatile mothers. Some couples fight, we mostly pretend stuff never happened.

The new me was happy, excited for possibilities, and acutely aware of what issues were mine and what issues were not. Standing in our kitchen in cycling gear, my husband was telling me what I was thinking. While it may have been a match to the me of two weeks before, it was not the me post-Carefree. "That's not at all what I'm thinking," I said, patting myself in an attempt to convey that the words he was saying weren't on me anywhere. It takes very little for my husband to feel cornered. When he does, he reacts defensively and rapidly. No matter how many years we've known each other, that energy always catches me off guard, often knocking the breath out of me. I typically back down, try to find a calm approach, or let it pass.

This time though, he met the roar of a tiger! I said with conviction, "those are your thoughts, not mine." When he responded with more anger, I saw the tiger take an energetic swipe at him. The energy was so intense he took a few steps backward.

I stood calmly and solidly in myself, for the first time in a very long time!

He went off on his bike ride, then retreated into the basement with a beer and a blanket. Yes, I did think about leaving him there! Instead, I went down with a compassionate heart (and a sleeping tiger) to explain that the new me had no space in her heart for blame and resentment.

* * *

A few days later, the tiger helped me clear out deeply rooted, intense emotions of anger, rage, and fury around an old relationship. In the middle of the clearing, she woke up and, with blazing speed, snatched an energy ball of emotions from the air and popped it into her mouth! It was such an intense emotional release I passed out on the couch for a restorative catnap.

In my next meditation, the tiger got up from her slumber, casually ambled out the left side of my diaphragm, and gave me another flick of her tail as she disappeared from view.

* * *

As this story unfolded, it allowed me to see how many small changes and decisions to overcome myself led to greater conviction around who I was becoming. Let's connect the dots to uncover how I was able to embrace a new kind of personal power.

1. My unconscious conversation left me feeling uneasy or out of alignment.
2. To get back into alignment, I decided how I now wanted to be with people.
3. I reminded myself that I would never want to speak from a platform of spiritual arrogance.
4. I owned my behavior and apologized, even though the person was not holding any energy around the situation. The apology was actually for me, to me!
5. The BEC meditation cleared out some old patterns around feeling powerless.
6. The clearing made space in my solar plexus energy center, which is associated with "personal power, self-esteem, and directed intention[20]."
7. The tiger was the perfect symbol to walk into the open space. When my new self was tested, the tiger helped me stand in my power.
8. The tiger stayed until I could resolve a deep inner conflict, chomping on the energetic release like it was catching a bird.

* * *

Who Am I Now?

Standing in my power was very new to me then. I met the force of another person's anger and held my ground, knowing their emotions were not mine to take on. The energy sent by them bounced back with a force that they could feel physically.

Once the tiger and I resolved the deep-seated anger around my old relationship, power started to change for me. My foundation of safety seemed to make it stronger than it was before; immovable, yet softer and more compassionate. It's a force of high-frequency love that easily repels lower vibrational frequencies.

* * *

I was talking a walk on a windy spring day, close to completing the draft of this book, pondering whether I dared to write about Spiritual Arrogance. While meandering along with my dog, I started writing a book outline in my head, debating with myself over the potential controversy I might cause if I shone a spotlight on the incongruence of many spiritual teachers. Would the people behind the scenes step forward and say publicly what they'd been telling me privately? Should I share those untold stories of abuse of power so people could learn how to connect with and TRUST their own inner teacher?

I asked the universe for a clear sign.

A few hours later, things were still milling around in my brain, so I decided to jot down some preliminary ideas and outline notes. When I opened my computer to start a new file, the first one listed was, *What to do When a Tiger Walks Into Your Meditation*. I hadn't touched that file in months, what was it doing at the top? Curious, I clicked it open, thinking, "why did I take that chapter out? I love that story!"

I was blown away when I saw this:

> *I could write an entire book from this one chapter! I admit it. I can get on a soapbox about spiritual arrogance.*
>
> *I've spent a lot of my life believing others had access to special places I wasn't good enough or evolved enough to go. I've also met a lot of people who truly believed they did have access to special places others weren't good enough or evolved enough to go.*

Perhaps it was time for my Tiger to return? To embrace her passion and presence. To step out of the shadows and stand gracefully and firmly in the pure light of truth.

Within hours of my morning walk, I'd had a conversation with a friend who helped me move the energy I had around my personal disappointment with spiritual arrogance. After that cleared, I wrote the majority of this section and called Karen Kessler.

***

Karen's influence is peppered throughout this book. Years ago, she walked up to me at a women's networking event, and a friendship evolved that was very different for me at the time. Our relationship is effortless because we want each other to shine as brightly as possible. If one of us gets into a hole, it doesn't matter how much mud and crap is in there; one will pull the other out. We carry no attachment to the story of how we ended up in the mire, choosing to explore possibilities for how to teach what we just learned to others.

Karen is also super fun! She brings curious kid energy to every conversation, giggles often, and does this thing that leaves me in complete awe. I'll share an experience, and she gives me the words to explain it from her vast reservoir of knowledge. We call her the Universal Translator.

In our phone call, Karen helped me connect to the purpose of the new book, which allowed me to see possibilities from a higher viewpoint. The topic of spiritual arrogance changed from controversial subject matter to one that could alter perception, which was not what I'd thought mere hours earlier!

***

This is how fast I receive clarity and guidance when I get focused. Here's what I do:

1. Align my energy.
2. Ask well-crafted questions.
3. Let go of expectation.
4. Be open to answers.

Did you notice how I had to be open to being off base about my original premise? By opening the computer file, I'd received a confirmation for writing a book with my old interpretation of spiritual arrogance. I could have stopped when I found the Tiger Chapter and called it a sign from the universe...which it was.

Throughout the day, I allowed myself to be guided in a way that connected me to the deeper truths of spiritual arrogance. Even though it meant letting go of a really great original idea.

Letting go allows for something more significant to arrive. And more keeps coming when we stay open.

* * *

What are the "Geo Shape Things"?

Those *"geo shape things"* that I mentioned in the Journal Entry are something I see all the time and are called fractals. Turns out fractals aren't just random colors and shapes of an overactive imagination. In science, they are the building blocks of all matter, making them the first visible sign that our thoughts are becoming material. In 2018, Dr. Joe began to teach about fractals, which was so exciting to me as it helped validate how I'd been creating my life.

In 2015 though, I'd considered the arrival of these colorful geometric shapes my gifts for having overcome an aspect of myself that no longer wished to travel with me.

Turns out, that is also the truth.

Those orange/deep pink/yellow fractals with the soft edges were the building blocks of my new life, gently falling into my open, receptive space.

* * *

To receive a free gift from Karen Kessler of ChooseRESULTS Inc. that she created specifically for Carefree readers, go to resources.adwynna.com Chapter 19.

20

The Song of your Soul

It's amazing how powerful music is, and to think I have all that power in the palms of my hands!
  Craig Young 12-10-2018

In the fall of 2013, I was in a holding pattern, waiting for a company I was involved with to open in Canada. For some reason, I decided to work the morning shift at my local tennis club. For slightly over minimum wage. I also got to play tennis for free. My job included opening up in the morning, getting players signed in, answering the phone, and balancing the books. Sounds easy enough. The clubhouse was an old and very tired school trailer, and I was the only employee there first thing, which meant I also shoveled snow, dealt with restroom issues, and the occasional leak.

I had no idea why I'd said yes to this!

Craig Young operates the tennis club through a complicated leasing arrangement, and the facilities are temporary until the owners build on the property. I'd met Craig years prior, and his rather weak handshake and poor eye contact left me with the impression that he wasn't particularly confident. Still, he seemed like a decent guy when I applied for the job, and he was grateful to have me on board.

Craig turned out to be quite the surprise package!

He'd come into the Club a few times a week, and we started chatting about the books he listened to while he drove. I'd read many of them, and he was thrilled to have someone to talk to who shared his interests. He often spoke of his family and mentioned some issues his son was having.

* * *

I was in full hide myself mode then, but after a few weeks of listening to this poor kid's struggles, I got brave, opened my mouth, and told Craig a little bit about my other life. When I showed him how I work with clients right there in his office, his mouth dropped open, and the light bulb went on.

Craig is the person who pulls the most through me so it can land here on earth. From the day he discovered we were two peas in a pod, he's asked me at least 2000 questions!

When he first started working with me as my client, he had a frozen left shoulder and pain in his right knee. These were keeping him from biking and running, and he certainly couldn't hit a tennis ball anymore. Over time, I discovered that Craig didn't want to be hitting tennis balls at all. In fact, he really wanted to be more hands-off at the tennis club so he could pursue his many other interests.

And his most significant other interest is music. Craig was a closet musician, secretly composing songs in a tiny section of his basement surrounded by a mountain of kids toys. He was reluctant to perform in front of others even though he'd been in a band when he was younger. Music as a career had been tossed in the dead-dream pile of firewood, along with a few other twigs he can share someday.

* * *

Craig and I are now close friends, and we have shared many experiences together, including a few Dr. Joe events. He sort of reminds me of the boy next door who has the coolest ideas for adventures. You know the one? The kid your parents secretly wish would move away because you're always coming home with scuffed knees and creepy bugs in jars? He has this mischievous energy and is incredibly funny.

Craig's three kids call me Aunt Wynna, and I adore his entire family. These days he cycles and runs and recently needed to be reminded he once had a frozen shoulder. He has a manager who runs the tennis club and excellent staff who make it enticing for him to go into work.

He bought a grand piano and made a bigger space in the basement for creating music. He has written music for people all over the world and even got tapped to compose a trailer for a TV show.

Along the way, he discovered his unique and awe-inspiring gift. The ability to connect in and compose your unique Soul Music! This freaked him out at first, but once he started sharing the compositions, the feedback blew him away.

He now knows your soul music changes as you evolve, giving him countless opportunities to provide us with the sound of our always expanding self. How cool is that?

Who Am I Now?

I've learned so much from this man. His questions have made me realize what I know and have challenged me to allow more answers to come through me and onto the page.

Stay Open. Focus on the side effects. Be grateful.

He saw so much in me that I took for granted. Stuff he knew people like his old-self needed.

He's pushed, prodded and encouraged me to be me and I am forever grateful.

So, this is more like *Who is Craig Now?*

Ever notice how the years blur into one long moment when you're finally enjoying them?

* * *

Craig didn't jump in and start doing what he's now doing the first month after his aha moment in his office. Five years ago, the things he would say out loud that he wanted were directly proportional to what he believed was possible. The rest were secret dreams with no color or detail…or belief!

What did he initially want? To resolve his frozen shoulder and bum knee. To have his son sleep more so everyone else could sleep more.

Open the door to wanting, and other things pop out.

It seemed it would be helpful for him to have less tension at the tennis club and more freedom to pursue his creative interests.

Keep asking for that vision to expand, build trust, gain confidence, and then he's wanting a music career that replaces his tennis income and kicking Type 1 Diabetes.

What did he do? Who has he become?

He stayed open, tried new things, learned more, and yes, asked even more questions. His vision of what was possible grew and grew. And then it grew some more. It's still expanding, and that is what keeps us alive and vibrant.

Craig kept embracing more and following every clue. Like the rest of us, some things happened quickly, some had a lot of resistance. He went to a Dr. Joe Progressive workshop and didn't meditate for a year! Then he started slowly, meditating a few minutes a day in nature. Now he meditates daily and takes those long cold showers a la Wim Hof. He's never been healthier!

* * *

Although I was part of this journey and worked with him, many of his breakthroughs happened because he took a recommendation, followed his own guidance, and developed new relationships.

No matter who you read or follow, you still have to do your own work. And Craig's story demonstrates how rapidly your life can change once you start.

Craig really kicked things into high gear in early 2017, which was about three years after we started working together. It's like he wrote the song of his soul as he was, then edited out the parts that didn't work, kept mixing in the elements that did and poof... everything went exponential!

By the time he walked into the Dr. Joe Advanced Follow Up workshop in the summer of 2018, the first three people he had introduced himself to said something like, "oh, you're the Music Man!" I'd find him on breaks, and he always had people around him. He was engaged, enjoying himself, and was bold enough to walk up and chat with Dr. Joe about his music before receiving a Coherence Healing!

Now his compositions are being played at Dr. Joe's events. He was inspired to write a piece of music called *A State of Grace* after his experience with Coherence Healings. Guess what? When he sent it into the Dr. Joe team, that is precisely what they used it for.

You cannot make this stuff up!

* * *

What guided me to send an email to Craig, saying, "I'd like to work for you?" It wasn't the job or the money. I just needed to fill some time, and it seemed easy enough to do. Or so I told myself. What I really needed was a mischievous angel to pull all of the knowledge and experience of my lifetime out of me and into the world!

Who could have guessed how elegantly the universe was working in our favor?

This story will continue, of course. It has so many elements and an enormous ripple, and yes, we know many of you are all...what about Craig's son? What about the diabetes?

His son totally has a story worth telling, and someday we will ask him to do just that. For now, he is a thriving pre-teen with an ingenious imagination. To the amazement of all, his refusal to conform to anyone's definition of a regular kid opened the door for all of us to step into our power, see beyond our limitations and let go of constrictive beliefs. Quite the mission for a young boy! As for the diabetes? Well...

...like all great pianos...you'll have to stay tuned.

* * *

If you are curious, you can listen to my conversation with Craig Young about *Soul Music*, or download a free song at resources.adwynna.com

21

Truth Evolves

I know I know nothing; those that know, do. Lessons at once both misleading and true.
    Meaghan Horsley, *Thieves of Fire* 09/12/2012

Nothing is true. It's all true.

I wrote those words in 1995. This was my first inkling that the gem called truth has an infinite array of facets. I may believe I see an entire sparkling diamond, yet I only perceive this tiny speck on the lower right corner. When we are open to more, we continually expand our awareness, which then contributes to the perpetual expansion of the universe.

Over time I've become less convinced there are absolute truths. Even though the love of oneness is the truth, the way I experience oneness and understand oneness changes each time I have another experience of the love of oneness.

TRUTH EVOLVES

Accepting this concept is difficult in a society that values the right answer. From the minute we're born we're taught the names of things and how to identify them. The grass is green, the sky is blue, and these are your fingers and toes. We now know that children who were raised in isolation from society, or by a color-blind parent, can emerge at some point saying the grass is what we call blue, and the sky is what we call green.

Let's say our parents did their very best to teach us head and shoulders, knees and toes, some A, B, C's and 1, 2, 3's. Then we go to school and learn more facts, which turn out to be the approved version of the facts of the local school board, which may contain a boatload of fiction and leave out entire swaths of events that verifiably happened.

We are rewarded or punished for our ability to recall facts on tests, and mostly discouraged from asking questions. The kids who master facts and accept what's presented get positive attention, which then turns into prizes like college scholarships and high paying jobs. Some kids go down other tracks, valued for their athleticism, artistry, or musical abilities. Everyone is put in a box and neatly labeled. The kids who get other labels are often medicated, in the hopes that their label can change into one that is more acceptable.

Honoring the true essence of each individual seems to be outside the box of our current educational systems and employers. Yet, until we UnLabel all of us, we will continue to live in divided nations.

Many of you may think of math and science and tell me that answers found there are absolute truths. Of all the subjects, science should be the one most likely to evolve. Yet, this is not true, either!

* * *

I'm not going to not delve into topics that scientists have explained more clearly. If you are open to proof about the nature of truth, I'd suggest you dig in more. Try a 2018 release called *Mind to Matter, The Astonishing Science of How Your Brain Creates Material Reality* by Dawson Church. It's easy to understand, contains an astonishing number of references to scientific studies, and has extra resources for the deeply curious at the end of each chapter.

The scientist who originally opened my mind to truths that were being buried is Gregg Braden, the earth scientist, teacher, and author. Many years ago, I got dragged to a talk by Gregg at a small local church. There might have been 40 people sitting in the pews. These days Gregg speaks to audiences of thousands and has written 10 books.

That night in the small church, I learned some startling truths around science in the last 50-100 years.

Simply put. New science is not replacing old science. New truth is not replacing old truth.

Proven, peer-reviewed discoveries and new conclusions from re-running older experiments have been buried.

* * *

An easy topic to understand is the misconception that we have a finite number of brain cells (neurons) that are incapable of regenerating. Not true! Neurogenesis is the process by which new neurons are formed in the brain, and it happens throughout your life. It was discovered in 1965 and was accepted as truth in 1998. Yet my kids were still taught in high school in the 2000s that their brain cells were finite and would die off. What a great way to instill the fear that you'd better not do anything risky in your life. If messed up your brain with a sports injury or smoking pot, then you had NO chance of ever operating with an optimal mind.

How does that encourage us to live a life of exploration?

It turns out that every cell in our body continuously regenerates, meaning we are perpetually renewed. The first time I heard the truth about cell regeneration was during a Deepak Chopra lecture. I didn't understand much of the talk, but one gold nugget of truth launched me on a quest for answers to this question:

"If our cells regenerate constantly, **how** *do we get them to regenerate healthy?"*

That question was finally answered when I read. *You Are the Placebo.* Finally, someone was giving me the **how** for an issue that had burned in the back of my brain for almost 20 years! Rather than another book telling me to be afraid of everything in my environment while trying to sell me on another diet, or a pile of supplements and food restrictions I was presented with **scientific proof** that all of the technologies we need to heal ourselves and create fulfilling lives is designed into the human body.

So, that's what it means to go within!

Who Am I Now?

Gregg Braden states clearly in *Human by Design*[21], "New Discoveries Mean a New Story." He is referring to new information replacing old information on a global and scientific level, and it starts with our own stories. We must allow for truth to evolve, and the only way to do so is to let go of what we thought was true yesterday or even five minutes ago.

The need to be right is deeply ingrained in our psyches. After all, being right is how we've been rewarded our entire life.

**

Despite what your mother told you, it is freeing to develop the ability to let go of that which doesn't serve you anymore. You do not have to lie in your uncomfortable bed forever just because you made it 20 years ago with a bedspread you now can't stand.

We are, for the most part, OK with our tastes in bedding changing over time. We are not as OK with changing our beliefs. Why? Because we rarely take them out of the closet, put them on the bed, and say, "wow, I actually used to think like that?"

What I believed was possible 20 years ago does not resemble what I know is possible now. Does that make the me of 20 years ago wrong or stupid or a failure? No one reading this is going to say "yes" to that question, but I'm willing to bet you spend a considerable portion of every day beating the crap out of yourself for where you aren't.

When I work with clients, when I do my own inner work, I see how hard we are on ourselves for decisions we made in the past. Guilt, regret, and shame are our silent killers because these are the emotions we hide. From the world, and from ourselves.

I invite you to ask yourself, "Who am I now?" "Who am I becoming?"

There is power in those two simple questions.

**

Who I Am Now changes regularly for me, yet the core of me is the same beautiful light I've always been, even when I couldn't see her. As I uncovered myself and peeled away layers of resentment, anger, guilt, and shame, I realized I truly loved and deeply appreciated every iteration of myself.

Even when I was judging myself for not being where I wanted to be, I was being guided to this very moment.

May 12, 2015-Journal Entry
I woke up this morning and realized...I am happy.
I feel so very blessed, so vibrant, so alive.
So much info flows, I wonder how my pen will ever capture it all. Ideas, fun, wishes for others.
There is no more second, third, fourth guessing. It comes to me from the perfect place of fruit in the grocery store to an idea, to an interaction with a person. Each is perfect.

Time expands because things happen quickly.

I've not used coupons, don't care what food costs. If it's green, or speaking to me, I buy it. I eat so little the cost no longer matters.
I've eaten no chocolate, no sweets, really. Had a piece of apple crumble because my daughter made it.
Bread is disgusting and tasteless and heavy. Love fruit, veggies, protein.
I used to constantly eat cheese – connected now, no need.
Coffee is gone.
Water, lots of pure, delicious water, tastes amazing and goes down easily. No forcing myself to remember to drink it and half gagging.
I walk like I saw in my meditations. I glide, I'm elegant, and I feel beautiful.

CAREFREE, IT STARTS WITH OPEN

I do not see myself as I am in the mirror, I see myself as I am becoming.

* * *

To read Thieves of Fire *by Meaghan Horsley, or check out the 1995 version of Truth Evolves go to* resources.adwynna.com

22

Who Am I Now?

To breathe, to dream, to fly
　　Through worlds and crossing Time

Teacher, Master, Keeper, Mother

On your wings I would ask
　　You take me where I need to go

From your heart, I would ask
　　You teach me what I need to learn

Teacher, Master, Keeper, Mother

Hold my stories for a time
　　Hold my heart entwined with thine
　　And when our Time is whole and nigh
　　Mother, teach me how to fly
　　Meaghan Horsley, 2017

When I talk to people about the guidance I receive, whether it comes in meditations or nature or conversations or a podcast or whatever I am open to, they often think messages arrive fully formed. Perhaps they believe a download from the divine is like a business plan or a pretty vision board that comes with a map of the rest of my life. While it sometimes happens with the clarity us humans would prefer, more often than not, I get glimpses and pieces that lead to more and more and deeper levels of understanding.

Which pretty much describes how we learn anything new here in the physical world. The day I decided to pick up a tennis racquet, I wasn't hitting winners. I was happy to hit two balls in a row and not trip over my own feet!

I would describe what I receive in meditations as more of an unveiling. It's not that my guides are deliberately being cryptic, and I do not believe the universe tests us.

I have to get used to the new level before I can open into and receive the next one.

As annoying as it is, I've learned that the only way to make a new habit become second nature is to recognize, accept and surrender to this statement: I just might suck at something I'd previously been good at before the higher level kicks in.

I had to be able to hit a ball over the tennis net, have it land in the court, and do that consistently before I could whack a ball with more pace. Then I had to reliably hit with speed and still have it land in the court. I added new shots and improved my technique. And on it goes…*provided* I'm willing to invest in my tennis game and live with the ebbs and flows associated with taking my game to the next level.

* * *

WHO AM I NOW?

When our future-self doesn't show up right away, many of us stop or are content to stay put. There are the usual comparisons we make with other people. Voices in our head saying things like:

- *Damn it, she just started, and she's so much better than I am already.*
- *How will I ever catch up?*
- *They must have more natural talent than I do.*
- *I've never been good at things like this.*
- *I tried this before and failed.*
- *Maybe I don't really want this.*
- *I'm too old to learn something new.*
- *I'm too young to master this.*
- *And all the blah, blah's we have blahing around in our heads that we use to stop us in our tracks.*

Meditation quiets those voices. It also has tons of other well-documented benefits, and to me, a mind without chatter is worth every frustration we encounter while meditating. I see so many people stop before they ever really start, whether that's meditation, getting fit, or eating better. A noisy mind will talk you out of your future-self, a quiet mind will open you to possibilities.

* * *

Being open also means I get to let go of thoughts I once believed or behaviors that used to work for me. It's become fun to say good-bye to programs and patterns.

Since the day I was told to "go play now," I've been to magical places and had extraordinary things happen. In and out of meditation! I've met so many inspiring, heart-centered people, each of them with dreams and ideas and a desire for connection. I love waking up every day, wondering what gifts are coming to surprise and delight me.

Do I ever get caught off guard by what my guidance reveals? Absolutely! I'd thought Carefree and all that followed was a WOW of a lifetime. How could it get better than that?

Well, keep asking that question, and you will find out for yourself.

I kept asking questions, continued learning, did my daily meditations, and above all, I remained open to possibilities. I received answers I'd been seeking around my work, my mission, and my passions. I'd come so far in my life since the day I'd left for Carefree. I was calm, healthy and happy. I'd let go of contracts and volunteer responsibilities to make space for the new me. I'd expanded my inner circle, so I had clients and great friends. I felt like I was ready to launch programs and books and take myself out into the world. Yet I wasn't producing a website or compiling my books for public consumption.

What was going on?

* * *

In mid-2018, I went looking for a journal entry to add to a chapter. Instead, I found this:

> Sunday, October 25, 2015
>
> I get very excited about writing. A year ago, next weekend, I drove thru rain, sleet, hail, and snow to Norwalk (Dr. Joe Progressive Workshop)w/a thousand voices in my head screaming inner obscenities at me about my general level of loserness.
>
> I guess, well, I know actually, that many of the people I admire

and follow have haters.

We reach the ones who can hear our voice. I will reach the ones who can hear mine.

I may say what has already been said a thousand times, and one person will finally hear it because it arrived for them in a way they could receive it.

(I kept writing for a while, noting that I was aware I was being told to write. Eventually, my pen began moving on its own...)

Over to you Tracey *(my deceased sister)*

Dwyn..." *yes, Tracey,*" Dwyn you've gone way too quiet. You need to make some noise, shake things up, make things happen. Get writing, keep writing, never stop writing. For God's sake, read what you write once in a while!

(Which is hilarious because I'd totally forgotten about writing this!)

"Ok sis, is that it?"

No, Dwyn, that's not it. You are golden, pure light, and you need to start showing up that way every damned day.

"Really, Trace, damned?"

Shut up, Dwyn, and listen. You have let your crazy ass head talk you out of being who you bloody well know you are.

"Hey, I thought you angelic types don't judge or get frustrated with us mortals?"

F&$@ that Dwyn. We'll talk to you in any language you can actually hear.

"Alrighty then."

Seriously Dwyn, you are driving yourself bonkers for no reason. You know enough, stop with the endless downloads. You are enough. You have straight access to me, Auriel, and the entire kingdom of archangels, guides, and light beings!

"Ok. I get it. So when I set an intention, do I set it, or do I ask for guidance to set it?"

Ask for guidance, because we know what you want in its purest form. We are very acquainted with your everything you've asked for. It's all here, and you put it here so we can help pave the way for you to receive it. And Dwyn, some of it, some of what you've asked for – you're already over it. You wanted it, and now you really don't. That's cool. Totally ok. It might still arrive, fine for you to just give it away.

"Ok, anything else?"

Nope, you're at the end of a page, and I know you like things tidy. HA!

"Thanks, T – love you."

* * *

That's what was going on! I was refusing to be publicly the very person I am now. I was writing this book, while trying to hide the mystical parts. I have more than enough life experience to write a compelling book series, but that wasn't what my guidance (or my sister) was telling me.

I was being guided to write truth.

To be the *"living example of truth."*

To help others access their truth.

* * *

The most consistent message I've had from guides is to *write*. My sister Tracey pops in often. As you've just read, she's there to kick my butt, and early on hers was a presence (or energetic signature) I could easily recognize.

By 2018 the messages to write were persistent, varied, and often quite amusing. I'd been given a purple pen with a purple feather on it from Dr. Wayne Dyer during a walking meditation on a beach in Cancun in 2016, which was an unexpected gift and more than enough encouragement. Imagine my astonishment when that *exact purple feather* dropped from the sky and landed at my feet in a park near Toronto eighteen months later.

I was utterly overcome with emotion over one tiny, fluffy feather. The people with me were absolutely bewildered; watching me jump up and down with delight, laughing and crying at the same time.

Turns out Wayne Dyer always wrote with a pen and paper, which allows more of our divine guidance to flow. I wasn't a big follower while he was in his physical body, yet Wayne drops in on me often since his surprise appearance on that Mexican beach. He's usually handing me that pen, encouraging me to write, and we joke around about the day he will let me wear his signature black hat.

* * *

In August 2018, I attended a Dr. Joe Advanced Follow Up workshop in Amelia Island, Florida, called Dreamtime II. It had an unusual format and a very relaxed and open Dr. Joe. The people I met were thrilled to be there, mostly because they could also relax and be themselves. My flight home was delayed, and I ended up having a deep conversation at the airport with someone from the workshop.

> It struck me how many of us are hiding who we are after we leave the safe confines of an event. It also struck me that the world is being deprived of our gifts of beauty, love, healing, and insight!

On the flight home, I made a decision to come out of hiding. I finally connected to the purpose of openly sharing my story. Every day, I help people open to their power. I help them access the very person they know they are and are afraid to be. And if I'm guiding them, assuring them that it's safe and magical and fulfilling to be who they are, I had to do it too!

I had to become a living example of truth, even if speaking my reality meant opening myself to mockery and disbelief.

They are not my audience.

You are.

My vision is to transform the lives of as many people who are open to my voice.

And if you are the one person this book helps, then everything I've ever experienced, each choice I've made to overcome myself that brought me to a greater version of me, has been, as Dr. Joe always says, "totally worth it."

* * *

Endings are always new beginnings. Ask yourself these questions often;

- *What is "it" that I want?*
- *How will I start to bring "it" into my life?*
- *Am I open to receiving "it"?*

And our hearts now know with absolute certainty;

"It" always, endlessly, and ever so happily, starts with open...

* * *

June 6, 2015-Journal Entry

The changes in me are profound and lasting. I know this is only the beginning, yet what I have is already more than enough. So much more.

Before Carefree, I had created a life of beauty and could not feel it. I could see it, off in the distance, but it could not land. Yet, I persisted in my creation. I never gave up. I kept my faith. I believed everything, all things, things bigger than my ability to ever imagine are possible. Not just possible, but REAL and on a train heading to my station.

These days I'm happy to take that train and let the day unfold. There is pure joy in each moment and, because I'm paying attention, the universe continually surprises me.

I have no idea what the future truly holds. I do see that a sprinkle of fairy dust here, a beam of light into a tiny fissure, can nudge aside old wounds, doubts and fears.

I know love and allowing and holding space for myself and others really does work. Just let go of how they appear to be now, or who I expect them to be.

When we see ourselves and others as whole, we can step forward into our future selves –– embracing the light of who we really are.

Epilogue

Outside, it's 104° Fahrenheit, and the haze from wildfires has hidden most of Mount Hood. I'm in Portland, Oregon, for a Dr. Joe Advanced Follow-Up (AFU) with Leanne, my blue-eyed friend, and Craig. It's the first meditation of the event, and it's not going well. I'd brought my expectations of prior workshops into the room with me and found my mind searching for known experiences. It's about 6:30 am, and I'm mentally beating myself up because I haven't been whisked off by dragons into other realms or encountered any light beings. My thoughts are scattered and I'm already predicting my outcome of this being a not-as-good-as some other workshop. All based on a few minutes of mind chatter!

It's times like this when doing The Work pays off.

I take a deep breath and decide to enjoy the moment, feeling gratitude for being there, reminding myself that there is a whole weekend ahead of me. I release my expectations, breathe energy into the room, love on all the people, enjoying the music, and the familiar sound of Dr. Joe's voice.

I move into a feeling of peace, and surrender into the meditation, allowing whatever happens to happen. Content with the knowledge that nothing might happen at all, enjoying the energy moving through my body.

A couple of hours later, the meditation is winding down. I'm lying on

EPILOGUE

the cold, cement floor in the basement of the hotel in Portland, freezing from the air conditioning, dreaming of standing in the heat just outside those doors. Relaxing fully into the final moments, drifting away to the place between wakefulness and sleep.

Suddenly, I'm in the event room in Carefree as it looked on May 1, 2015. I'm up high in the corner when I spot Adwynna sitting in a chair at the back of the room with an EEG cap on her head. She's beside a brain map technician, with her head and arms resting on a table.

And I'm so in love with her.

My body is flooded with intense feelings of admiration and joy as I observe her. I'm in awe of her resilience, her courage, her beautiful heart. The intensity of the emotions I have for my former-self causes tears to stream down the face of my current-self.

As I watch Carefree Adwynna, I become aware that she is checking on people, finding them in the ether, making sure they are OK, sending them love. Her heart is wide open, so I start to speak…

Dwyn, everyone is safe. You are safe, everyone in your world is safe…

Gifts & Gratitude

Books do not write themselves, and authors do have occasional meltdowns. Since mid-2015, when "It Starts With Open" revealed itself as the name of this book, I have had the absolute joy of being supported by a diverse group of talented, generous people.

Thank you.

Thank you for helping me shape the vision of this book. Thank you for believing in me when I wavered. Thank you for your insights, your brilliance, your guidance.

I have deep admiration for Arlene Pe Benito, Willa Mavis, Meaghan Horsley, Karen Collacutt, and Bradley Charbonneau. They read and edited my many drafts, provided feedback, asked for clarity, and fixed my comma splices. Many offered, you came with red pens!

For Bradley. You were there when the title dropped out of the universe; you were there when I was mostly talking about writing; you held my hand during the endless technology of publishing. You also held me together on the morning of my B'Earthday, and I'm forever grateful.

Anne Mitchelson, I cannot wait to write the story of how this book cover came to life! You tapped into a higher vision and gave me so much more than I'd ever seen on my own. The cover expertly captures the essence of the book, and I am thrilled to my core every time I look at it.

Meaghan Horsley, your many talents come from a place of deep connection, spilling onto these pages in the form of quotations and poetry and inspiration. You are the best sounding board, and your questions and insights have made me a better person.

Some of you are "characters" inside this book, so you know I love and appreciate you! Karen Kessler, my thanks for our weekly calls filled with magic and creation and insight. Jeannie and Leanne, my roomies from Carefree, you bring profound gifts to this planet so keep shining!

Writers live in the world of their book. I am grateful for the patience my family, who have seen me disappear for many hours, then emerge slightly fuzzy, yet functional enough to cook dinner!

There are so many incredible people in my life since Carefree! Two of my *new* friends had a significant impact on this book:

Joel Mitchell, your insights into who I am are reflected in these pages. Thank you for being the embodiment of peace and kindness and for the brilliance of our many, and varied PlayStorms.

Arlene Pe Benito, you magical woman! You dragged me out of the closet I'd been hiding in and made me proclaim my book in public. Thank you for bringing out the kid in me and happily being my playmate. I'm so excited for what's coming when we bring AccessU into the world!

* * *

And then there's **Dr. Joe Dispenza**, whose brilliant work has healed my heart, opened me to countless blessings and created a life of love and magic. Since 2015, I've gotten to know Dr. Joe on several occasions, volunteered for his workshops, and spent a week with him and a group exploring wine in Italy. He knows of this book, and I want to be clear that he hasn't yet read it, or endorse it. He does, "appreciate that it is a result of doing the work."

When I first started writing this book, my only interaction with Dr. Joe had taken place in Carefree when he walked by us as we were waiting to register. He'd just briefed the volunteers near the pool deck and was almost past us when he suddenly turned back and said, "I have to give you a hug. You just seem so darned happy!"

***The magic of Carefree had begun!*stop**

Notes

INTRODUCTION

1   Dispenza, Joe, Dr., *Becoming Supernatural, How Common People are Doing the Uncommon* (Hay House Inc., 2017)

PROLOGUE

2   There is a therapeutic state known as the stillpoint that can occur spontaneously. When a stillpoint is achieved, a person's craniosacral rhythm comes to a pause, inducing a state of deep relaxation that allows the fight-or-flight responses of the sympathetic nervous system to step down. This brings the healing and restorative powers of the parasympathetic system to the fore, liberating a wide range of self-correcting activity.

INTRODUCING: MY OLD SELF

3   The work of Dr. John Diamond can be found at www.drjohndiamond.com. *Life Energy, using the Meridians to Unlock the Hidden Power of Your Emotions* was first published in 1985 and remains one of the 5 books I would take to a deserted island. I always learn something new.

4   While researching the end-notes for this book I discovered that Kandis Blakely died in 2013 or 2014, depending upon what you read online. Some have continued with her work, some have modified it. At the time of this publication, I have no additional details.

THE LOST DECADE

5   Dr.   James L. Wilson www.adrenalfatigue.org/saliva-testing-for-adrenal-hormones/

6   Dispenza, Joe, Dr., *You Are The Placebo, Making Your Mind Matter* (Hay House Inc., 2014)

DIGGING IN

7   Dispenza, Joe, Dr., *Breaking the Habit of Being Yourself, How to Lose Your Mind and Create a New One* (Hay House Inc., 2012)

3D CREATION – CLIMB EVERY MOUNTAIN

8   Hawkins, David R. *"Power vs. Force, The Hidden Determinants of Human Behavior."* Hay House Inc., January 30, 2014. *Building on the accumulated wisdom of applied kinesiology (diagnostic muscle-testing to determine the causes of allergies and ailments) and behavioral kinesiology (muscle-testing to determine emotional responses to stimuli), David R. Hawkins MD, PhD has taken muscle-testing to the next level, in an effort to determine what makes people and systems strong, healthy, effective and spiritually sound.*

9   S.M.A.R.T is an acronym associated with goal setting. Goals are designed to be *Specific, Measurable, Assignable, Realistic and Time-based.*

10 I usually use muscle testing to identify and confirm what I need to work on, then I incorporate other modalities I've been trained in to change limiting beliefs or remove energetic patterns. For more information on those modalities, go to resources.adwynna.com

IS THAT AN EGG? - WEDNESDAY, APRIL 29TH

11 Mind Movies transforms a boring vision board into a fun, digital video vision board filled with positive affirmations, inspiring images and motivating music. www.mindmovies.com

OBSERVER - THURSDAY, APRIL 30TH

12 Heart Math Institute information www.heartmath.org

13 To watch the Derek Redmond video go to resources.adwynna.com

GRACE - FRIDAY, MAY 1, 2015

14 *"The energy centers in your body are centers of information. Each center has a plexus of neurons that correlates to a particular gland in your body."* The energy centers are explained in detail in Chapter 4 of *Becoming Supernatural.* and the Blessing of the Energy Centers meditations can be purchased at www.drjoedispenza.com

15 Dr. Jeffrey Fannin, Ph.D. www.thoughtgenius.com

MIRACULOUS - SUNDAY, MAY 3, 2015

16 From Wikipedia. The word "portal" in science fiction and fantasy generally refers to a technological or magical doorway that connects two distant locations separated by spacetime. It usually consists of two or more gateways, with an object entering one gateway leaving via the other instantaneously.

Places that are linked by a portal include a different spot in the same universe (in which case it might be an alternative for teleportation); a parallel world (interdimensional portal); the past or the future (time portal); and other planes of existence, such as heaven, hell or other afterworlds. A parallel world, such as the Wood between the Worlds in C. S. Lewis's Chronicles of Narnia, may exist solely to contain multiple portals, perhaps to every parallel world in existence.

Portals are similar to the cosmological concept of a wormhole, and some portals work using wormholes.

JOYOUS BEYOND CONDITION

17 Information on the Repossible Podcast can be found in the resource section for this book located at resources.adwynna.com

THE ABSENCE OF FEAR IS PEACE-MONDAY, MAY 4, 2015

18 Andrews, Ted. *Animal-Speak: the spiritual & magical powers of creatures great & small* (Llewellyn Publications, fifteenth printing, 1998)

19 Sams, Jamie & Carson, David, *Medicine Cards: the discovery of power through the ways of animals. Illustrated by Angela C. Werneke* 1988

WHAT TO DO WHEN A TIGER WALKS INTO YOUR MEDITATION

20 Chapter 4, *Blessing of the Energy Centers* from *Becoming Supernatural* by Dr. Joe Dispenza.

TRUTH EVOLVES

21 Braden, Gregg. *Human by Design, From Evolution by Chance to Transformation by Choice* (Hay House Inc. 2017)

About the Author

Adwynna MacKenzie is a speaker, author, and AccessU guide. For over 20 years, she has helped people access deeply hidden dreams and let go of what's been holding them back. She's written for publications and penned hundreds of human interest stories. Since her transformational breakthrough in 2015, Adwynna has embraced her natural abilities, and is passionately committed to helping us all shine our lights more brightly.

Carefree, It Starts With Open: An Invitation to Come Out of Hiding, and Embrace Your Super Natural Self is Adwynna's first book. The freedom of technology allows her to work with clients and write from anywhere in the world, so you never know where you will find her! To catch up with her latest adventures, visit her online at www.adwynna.com or on Twitter (@AdwynnaM).

You can connect with me on:

- http://resources.adwynna.com
- https://twitter.com/AdwynnaM
- https://fb.me/adwynnafanpage

Subscribe to my newsletter:

- http://carefree.adwynna.com

Also by Adwynna MacKenzie

Coming in late 2020! Book 2 of the Carefree Series.

A Return to Earth, Chapter 1

http://resources.adwynna.com

December 12, 2017 4:44am-Journal Entry

As I'm writing this, complete and utter calm has descended into my entire body and being.

I got up at 4:15am, went to the kitchen for water, and just stood at the window, watching the snow softly falling. We got 10-15cm of the light, fluffy stuff overnight, and the backfield is illuminated.

I'm in a bathrobe and barefoot on the cold tiles, just appreciating the stillness in my body. Empty of emotion, yet filled with all emotions at the same time.

This is serenity.

Closed my eyes to appreciate the moment, the feeling, the divinity. When I opened them, a deer walked onto the path between our yard and the field. Appreciating that deer, then two more wandered into view. They grazed peacefully, one running toward the other playfully kicking up fresh snow. I watched them for 10 minutes or so. They are still there, three deer gently luring me to new adventures.

Prior to going downstairs, I'd been awakened by energy moving in my body.

Unlike last night's violent agitation and releases, this energy arrived with feelings of opening. At first, I was highly aroused. I am embodying all in my physical and energetic bodies.

All of this is happening to me-I'm not doing a meditation per se (although I am in that state, of course). I'm lying in my bed and simply allowing it all in.

Light that feels like pure golden liquid, calm love is spreading through my hips and tailbone and first energy center. It's grounding into the earth, and my body is constantly adjusting and shifting as this new energy moves in.

This light is different than other light I've seen/experienced. It's more golden-almost like it needs more heft or substance to be in my body. The origin of this light is from far, far away land (just a name I call it from the movie Shrek!) where my/our spiritual ancestors originated from (saying mine, me and I feel so odd-like they are foreign terms from a language I spoke as a child).

It feels like purity. So calm, so clean, so clear.

And so natural.

I'm not highly emotional. It's like I've been waiting, and now it's here, and all is as it's supposed to be.

I am aware of my "new" guides. There are 5 (of course). I am one, I have 2 more on each side in balanced pairs.

I have grounded this light into this energy center and can feel it go from my tailbone area deeply, deeply into the earth, and she –my divine earth mother - takes a "big drink on this one" LOL. She receives the light, and we connect deeply and profoundly. We are now breathing together as one.

This isn't a download or a transmission. I wasn't actually doing anything. Just allowing and receiving.

Natural –honestly, it feels as natural as breathing to allow and integrate all of this vibration and light. Absolutely gorgeous!

Along the way, I do realize this is me, these are my guides now. We have arrived.

It's all happening in the lower energy centers. **Bringing the light home into body.**

As I began to prepare to get up (light work makes me very thirsty!), I am in gratitude for these experiences. My heart fills with heat and warmth and opens front and back. I am suffused with energy and feel the awareness of embodiment.

Nothing is an upgrade. It's all simply levels of awareness.

www.ingramcontent.com/pod-product-compliance
Lightning Source LLC
Chambersburg PA
CBHW020037120526
44589CB00032B/463